Mercy Within M

Mercy Within Mercy

Georges and Pauline Vanier and the
Search for God

Mary Frances Coady

DARTON · LONGMAN + TODD

First published in 2015 by
Darton, Longman and Todd Ltd
1 Spencer Court
140–142 Wandsworth High Street
London SW18 4JJ

ISBN 978-0-232-53189-3

A catalogue record for this book is available from the
British Library.

Phototypeset by Kerrypress Ltd, Luton
Printed and bound by Scandbook AB

For Pat Halpin FCJ

Contents

Acknowledgements   *ix*

Foreword by Sister Wendy Beckett   *xiii*

Introduction   *xvii*

1. The Door of the Heart: 1938-1942   1

2. Weakness Calling Forth Mercy: 1943-44   23

3. Thirsting for God: 1945-1952   45

4. More Deeply in God's Love: 1953-1967   77

5. The School of L'Arche: 1968-1972   103

6. With Empty Hands: 1973-1991   133

Notes   153

Acknowledgements

My biography, *Georges and Pauline Vanier: Portrait of a Couple*, followed the lives of the Vanier couple in the public service they rendered, both singly and together, during the many upheavals of the twentieth century. The present book has attempted to illuminate the contemplative inner life that formed the spiritual impetus of their actions and involvements.

Thanks are due first of all to the various archives where much of the material in this book was found: the Georges P. Vanier Fonds at Library and Archives Canada, Ottawa ON; the Ware Carmel Archives, Ware, Herts; the British Jesuit Archives, London; the Robert Lax Archives, St Bonaventure University, St Bonaventure NY.

Short sections of this book were published in an earlier form in *Mount Carmel* (January-March 2014) and *Spirituality* (January-February 2013, July-August 2014). I am grateful to the editors of these publications.

The book was given structure and form during the Fall 2013 semester when I was a resident scholar at the Collegeville Institute in Collegeville MN. I would like to express my gratitude to the Institute for the enriching environment and community provided there. Many thanks as well to the Access Copyright Foundation for financial assistance.

I am also grateful to Monsignor Roger Quesnel, who, shortly after the death of Pauline Vanier, was asked to open an investigation process into the lives of Georges and Pauline Vanier with a view to the possible introduction of their cause for beatification as a married couple. The present volume is not related to that process, but Monsignor Quesnel nevertheless shared with me his own material on the Vaniers, and I thank him for his generosity. I would also like to acknowledge the kind assistance given to me by Deacon Eugene Margeson of the Archdiocese of Ottawa. Anne MacCarthy, as well, has been an ongoing source of help and encouragement.

Many thanks to David Moloney, Helen Porter, and Will Parkes at Darton, Longman and Todd, who have worked to make this book see the light of day.

The late Benedict Vanier OCSO and the late Thérèse Vanier, who died within five weeks of each other in the spring of 2014, had before their deaths given me their full trust as I went about the task of writing about their family. I remain deeply grateful to them.

Finally, I extend my profound gratitude to Jean Vanier and Michel Vanier, for their generous co-operation in the preparation of this book.

'Have you had sight of Me, Jonas My child?
Mercy within mercy within mercy.'
– Thomas Merton, *The Sign of Jonas*

Foreword

I can well remember as a young nun, reading that the new Governor General of Canada, Georges Vanier, was a Catholic, a devout practicing Catholic, as was his beautiful wife, Pauline. The half was not told. To be a 'practicing Catholic', even a devout one, may only mean that one goes to Mass on Sundays, keeps the law of the Church, supports the parish and is generous to the poor; is in other words, a good person. But all of this can be relatively superficial. To be truly a Catholic is to surrender to Our Blessed Lord with complete love – to want only Him, to live, as St Paul says, 'in Christ'. Although I was happy in 1959 to know that the Vaniers were good Catholics, I cannot express the joy with which I learn now that they were real Catholics. They both lived always in the presence of God.

Moreover, it seems to have been a perfect marriage, each supporting the other and bringing the other to a fullness of life that might not otherwise have been possible. They were very different in temperament and in background. Georges was a stern man of duty, Pauline a charming but anxious extrovert. He gave her strength through his unshakable love; he believed she was necessary to him in his diplomatic work. It was her warmth and sweetness, her open-armed approach to people that drew him out of an introverted loneliness. Pauline, on the other hand, for all the joy that she gave those who knew her, was always racked by a sense of failure and inadequacy. Only in Georges's love and confidence, his palpable need of her, could she feel affirmed and free. Perhaps the loveliest evidence of the closeness of this marriage is the way Pauline brought Georges to a deeper understanding of the fatherhood of God. Stern and unyielding in virtue, he had been raised in a Jansenistic tradition of human sinfulness. He did not dare to go to Holy Communion more than once or twice a year. He saw God as the Supreme Judge and shrank in awe before Him. To his astonishment, Pauline went joyfully to Holy Communion every day, sometimes after a night of champagne gaiety. She had no doubts about God's tenderness and his longing to keep her holy through his love and his sacraments. It was only after seventeen years of marriage that she persuaded him to come with her to listen to a priest she thought spoke with power the message of God. Rather reluctantly Georges came and was bowled over by the discovery of the depth of God's love. So they complemented one another here too: her calling to prayerfulness balanced and reinforced by his calling to duty; and his awe of God set in the context of divine love.

I knew nothing of the deep spiritual life of the Vaniers, but I can remember noting that there were two extraordinary contemporary apostles, Jean Vanier and his sister Thérèse, who had the same surname. I did not then know that they were son and daughter of the Governor-General Vaniers, but it did strike me as both unusual and wonderful that two such God-driven people should come from the same family. What were their parents like, I wondered. Up till now the most striking example of saintly parents producing saintly children had been the Martin family in nineteenth-century France. All five daughters became nuns, one of whom is now known as St Thérèse of Lisieux. Modern attention is being directed to her father and mother, showing how the shy and anxious Zélie Martin (rather like Pauline Vanier in fact) who died young and heroically and her gentle, unobtrusive husband, who gave up his watch-making shop so as to give all his time to his daughters, deserve concentrated study. It was from them Thérèse learned to be a saint. This seems to be equally true for the Vaniers. Jean Vanier has given his life to L'Arche, a community that devotes itself to offering self-supporting homes to people with mental disabilities. It is an extraordinary work of charity. Thérèse Vanier gave up a prestigious profession as a haematologist to work with these same 'least of the brethren', those the world ignores and rejects. The Vaniers, like Jesus, cherish and respect those whom society would cast aside. Surely, one thinks, such a passion for the poor of Christ must have been learnt in the home.

This moving book shows that it was indeed learnt in the home. Georges and Pauline spent at least half an hour in prayer together every evening. They tried to be totally aware of God's presence. Anybody who has taught in schools knows the sorrow of finding children who know nothing of God or even of morality. Inevitably, it turns out that they have parents who do not know God either. Somewhere the rot must stop, and it can only be by teaching young people the truth about God and preparing them to have true marriages with homes in which the importance of love and truth and responsibility are fully accepted. There is very much about which we need to pray here, but such a book as this gives one great hope.

Sister Wendy Beckett
April 2015

Introduction

On 23 June 1945, Pauline Vanier, the wife of the Canadian ambassador to France, set out from Paris with her husband Georges and daughter Thérèse, to the town of Lisieux, most of which they found reduced to rubble from the Allied bombing of a year earlier. After they received greetings from the town's dignitaries, they were ushered to the Carmelite monastery, one of the few buildings still intact. There they were told that Mother Agnes of Jesus, the 84-year-old prioress, would see them.

Mother Agnes, the former Pauline Martin, had been the first of the Martin sisters of Lisieux to become a Carmelite. Marie had entered the monastery a few years later, and then, most famously, their 15-year-old sister, Thérèse, had joined them. After their father's death, a fourth sister, Céline, too, had become a Carmelite in the Lisieux monastery. Thérèse died in 1897 at age 24 and was canonized a saint 28 years later. Marie died in 1940, and so the only other Martin sister still in the Lisieux Carmel, besides Mother Agnes, was 76-year-old Céline, now known as Sister Geneviève.

───━━◆━━───

Of the Vaniers' four other children at this time, son Jean was in England and the others in Canada. In a collective letter to them, Pauline sets the scene at the Lisieux Carmel as she, her husband and daughter prepared to meet Mother Agnes: 'We were all very *émotionnés* at the thought of meeting this woman, a sister of the saint and a saint herself! Daddy saying, "you'll do the talking because I'm too frightened", and I saying, "Oh no! You must, I'm terrified." Thérèse saying, "Well, I know that I shan't say a word".

'We walked over to the Carmel with Msgr. Germain who left us at the door. We were taken by a "turn" sister to a parlour. Like all Carmel parlours, it has the grille with the spikes. But those spikes have no more terror for me now! I know them too well to be frightened. We waited, the three of us very nervous and wondering what we would say. Suddenly we heard a door handle turn, the door opening, a voice said, "Deo gratias" and we none of us knew what to answer, which is disgraceful as far as I am concerned! Then to our great surprise and great relief we saw the shutter open and there we saw this grand woman, old in years but young in spirit.'

Mother Agnes had brought her *conseil* with her, including – to the Vaniers' surprise and delight – the only other surviving sibling of St Thérèse, Sister Geneviève. The prioress was slightly deaf, and so voices were somewhat raised, 'but otherwise there was no difficulty whatsoever in the conversation. She took it in hand and we followed on.' The sisters told the Vaniers 'what a character' their young saint was, adding, '*Il n'y avait rien à l'eau de rose en elle*' ['There was nothing sentimental about her']. At another juncture, when

Pauline Vanier asked them to plead to St Thérèse on her behalf, Sister Geneviève waved her off: 'You know how younger sisters are – she never listens to me!'

'Then,' Pauline adds, 'I told [them] about Ganna [Pauline's mother] being Père Pichon's spiritual daughter … I told her about Hitchin[1] and how privileged I had been … She said that they would pray for our family very particularly and added, "*Vous êtes de la famille maintenant.*" ["You're part of the family now."]' By this time, 'we spoke on cheerily and without any more fear. Even Daddy launched himself in conversation about a parallel to be drawn between St Thérèse and St Jeanne d'Arc, which they all approved and Mother Agnes asked one of the Sisters to read out of a passage of the last words of St Thérèse in which she says that she wishes that she were a soldier.'

Pauline ended the collective letter: 'We came away feeling that St Thérèse was more than ever the protector of the family, more especially after the assurance of Mother Agnes's prayers. The whole thing is so closely linked.'[2]

With this visit, Pauline Vanier had in a sense come full circle. The Jesuit Almire Pichon, whom she referred to in her letter, had become close to St Thérèse's family, and the saint herself described him in her autobiography, *Story of a Soul*, as 'a director such as St Teresa desired'.[3] Père Pichon was sent to Canada as a retreat

preacher in November 1888 ('hardly had I been num-
bered among his children when he left for exile,'[4] the
saint writes).

In Montreal, where Père Pichon landed, he soon
met another young woman, who was a year younger
than Thérèse Martin. Her name was Thérèse de Salaberry. The Montreal Thérèse was an orphan who lived
at a convent school called   Pensionnat d'Hochalaga.
The exact circumstances of the meeting between Père
Pichon and Thérèse de Salaberry are not known, but
in some way he took on the role of 'spiritual father' to
the girl, and she in turn became devoted to him. As a
young Jesuit he had come under the influence of the
spiritual writing of St Francis de Sales, who, in *Introduction to the Devout Life* and other works, advocated a
gentle trust in God.

Père Pichon became known for encouraging an
affectionate attitude toward God, advocating a personal love of Jesus rather than a stern doctrinal approach or
an overly judgemental view of one's own unworthiness.
('Take Jesus by the heart' was an exhortation he liked
to use, and St Thérèse would eventually echo it.) He
also encouraged devotion to the Sacred Heart, which
he regarded as a means of discovering God's infinite
love through the heart of Jesus.

The parentless Thérèse de Salaberry, a young woman
in need of affection, was ripe for the kind of guidance
that Père Pichon offered. The Jesuit may have tried
to steer her toward the life of a nun, but she suffered
from fragile health and an anxious temperament and

probably would not have withstood the rigours of the cloister. At any rate, when she reached adulthood she married a man by the name of Charles Archer. When the Lisieux Thérèse died of tuberculosis in her Carmelite monastery on 30 September 1897, the Montreal Thérèse was three months pregnant. On 28 March 1898, she gave birth to a daughter, Pauline.

Thérèse de Salaberry Archer remained close to Père Pichon as her spiritual father, and as a young child, Pauline made her first confession to him. After his return from Canada to France in 1907, they kept in touch with him through correspondence and trans-atlantic visits until his death in 1919.

Pere Pichon's letters to Pauline's mother contained echoes of the advice he gave to thousands of other correspondents, sounding the same themes of God's mercy and trust in adversity: 'I ask you to be kind to your soul … Jesus is as kind toward it, as indulgent, as merciful, as you are sometimes hard and severe. Look after my daughter with tenderness, as a good mother looks after a suffering child. No vinegar! Pour on the honey.' 'Jesus is never more loving toward you than when he appears to be cruel. What a misfortune it would be if even for one day he suspended his merciful pursuit of you. Undoubtedly you have to walk like a blind person through thick darkness. But an invisible hand is leading you, supporting you, holding you, protecting you.' 'The path that God is making you follow is mysterious. But, even more, it's a path of mercy.' 'It seems that your heart's distress isn't over yet, that you still have something to learn from it. Jesus is busying himself in completing the lesson, and I see only a loving plan in it …' 'Against all appearances, believe in Our Lord's love *for you*. I can never emphasize this enough.'[5]

— · —

Pauline Archer was twenty-one years old when she met thirty-one-year-old Georges Vanier, recently returned to Canada from the war in France, who, on 28 August 1918, had lost his right leg in battle. They were both natives of Montreal and were married there in 1921. Pauline had grown into an extroverted young woman, with a need for affection and a tendency to anxiety similar to her mother's. Because of her health, her formal schooling was curtailed, and most of her education was conducted by governesses. As she grew into adulthood, she felt, from her mother's influence, a deep spiritual thirst and a desire for Christian service.

'You and I are going upward hand in hand toward the Light, because God is drawing us to Himself,' she wrote to her future husband a few days before their wedding. 'Our ambition must be to always set our sights on this summit. Nothing else matters. We mustn't forget that we were created for Him, and we must always show this with our lives. It will be our particular form of the apostolate.'[6] Georges's war wound had already taken a central place in their relationship: as an engagement gift he had given Pauline a small bottle, the size and shape of a perfume bottle, containing mud from the boot of his amputated leg. Each year on the anniversary of the date he was wounded, she would write him a letter of love and admiration.

But already, in the flush of youth and romance, she had set the tone for a lifetime of Christian service. Most of this service would take place in the world of diplomacy, in which the couple would become increasingly prominent. For nearly fifty years they would grow together in discovering God's love. Singly and together they would find a spiritual path that would take them deeper into their relationship with each other and with God.

By the mid-1930s Pauline, having come through a miscarriage and shaky early years of motherhood, would be open and ready for the spiritual adventure that would form a prayerful underpinning for the changes and turmoil ahead. During the coming years the Vaniers would be close to many of Europe's historical events and they would see their own children's lives unfolding in remarkable ways. Pauline would be led along a path remarkably similar to her mother's, one familiar to the Carmelites of Lisieux, and in his own time Georges would discover this path as well. Pauline's first guide would be an English Carmelite prioress, Mother Mary of the Cross.

Not surprisingly, the prioress's letters to Pauline can be seen to strike some of the themes that are to be found in Carmelite literature, and in particular those of St Thérèse's *Story of a Soul*.

In the second part of *Story of a Soul*, known as 'Manuscript B', St Thérèse writes of her discovery of 'the science of love' pouring out from God's mercy. The road leading to this discovery is the path of 'the surrender of the little child who sleeps without fear in its Father's arms.'[7] In a missive addressed to Jesus, she describes a dream in which Anne of Jesus, the founder of the Carmel in France, tells her 'He is content'. St Thérèse takes this as confirmation that the path of trust and sacrificial love she has been walking along—which eventually will be called the 'little way'—is acceptable to God, and this assurance is proof that she is loved. The dream is also a prelude to the many graces she asks for: elaborating on the various vocations that make up the Body of Christ (which she finds in the first letter of Paul to the Corinthians), she enumerates warrior, priest, apostle, doctor, martyr.

Then she moves on to 'the more excellent way', that of love.[8] This will be her vocation: to be love at the heart of the Church. She goes even further, offering herself as a 'victim' of God's merciful love, echoing the act of oblation she had made a year earlier. She declares herself as weak and powerless, and so her love will be proved by daily small sacrifices which she expresses to Jesus as the strewing of flowers (some of which will have thorns, she acknowledges) as if she were a child.

When one thinks of St Thérèse's affectionate nature, of her need to be loved and to give love, and her discovery that her vocation was to be love at the heart of the Church, one can see how Mother Mary of the Cross, perhaps more personally inclined to the loftier prose of St Teresa of Avila, is guiding Pauline Vanier. There is no mention of 'flowers' in the nun's letters (she refers only once to the younger Carmelite), and perhaps the floral imagery, cloying to modern sensibilities, does not appeal to her. Also, Mother Mary of the Cross is keenly aware of the Vaniers' circumstances: Pauline is not cloistered, but living through the joys and travails of marriage, motherhood and the vagaries of world events. Her days are lived against a larger immediate canvas than that of St Thérèse. She is very much in the world in a way that the saint, living in a cloister, was not.

But in their own way, in their particular time and place, Pauline and Georges too have a vocation at the heart of the Church. They may say with St Thérèse, quoting the Book of Wisdom, 'For to him that is little, mercy will be shown',[9] but instead of offering themselves as victim of God's merciful love, they can add, 'You do not ask for holocaust and victim; instead, here am I.'[10]

This open desire for God permeates everything that the couple sets out to do, and it can be seen in the letters Pauline writes to her children during the war years when the family is separated. (On 9 May 1944 she writes from Algiers to her eldest son: 'We are certainly living in interesting times and there is much for you young ones to do. You will need all the science of the knowledge of God that you can possibly have and you will have to have strength that alone He can give ... It is in prayer alone that one can find our needs. Not prayer of words, but prayer of the spirit. It is the awareness of God, as Fr Steuart calls it, that is essential. It is all the more difficult in these days of continuous agitation to stop and listen to Him and yet – how are we to reach Him if we don't listen? I find that the best time is just before going to sleep to try and do what Fr Steuart calls "pointing the spirit towards Him".'[11]) Always, against the backdrop of tension, anxiety and devastation, there remains the presence of God.

Throughout the whole of her long life, which will span most of the twentieth century, Pauline has both Martha's open-hearted spirit of generosity and Mary's longing to gaze upon God with love. Her temperamental anxiety, however, and the tendency to slide into depression, threaten to drag down her trust in God. She often feels unworthy – that her spiritual life is 'wrong' whenever her prayer seems nothing but a fog. She feels useless much of the time, as if her ambition to be of Christian service has frittered into nothing. As for her spiritual life, she can only often say with the psalmist, 'I have sought you with all my heart; let me not stray from your commands.' [12]

Mother Mary of the Cross's letters to Pauline span a period that is, in a sense, a time of exile for the Vaniers. By the time of the first letter, 5 January 1939, the couple have already passed an important turning point in their marriage and in Georges's spiritual life.

In the midst of the tumult of war, the family will eventually find itself scattered on three continents. Through all the daily upheaval, Pauline's Carmelite director exhorts her to loving abandonment, to letting go in recognition of God's mercy, to rejoicing before God in her weakness.

In the first part of *Story of a Soul* Thérèse says that Carmel was the desert where God wanted her to hide herself. Pauline's is a particular twentieth-century desert: her life and the lives of her family and all she comes into contact with are uprooted and in upheaval (though less tragically than millions upon millions of others) because of war. Her need for spiritual comfort finds a response from her Carmelite director who writes to her of simplicity and littleness. The prioress paraphrases the great St Teresa, but could equally be echoing the little St Thérèse: 'His Majesty loves to show His power in frail souls because in them His goodness meets with the least obstacle.' She repeats more than once the original Latin meaning of mercy: 'Miseri-cordare'—to give the heart to a wretched one.

In place of Thérèse's thorns, Mother Mary of the Cross refers to 'a zero temperature', which will recur in other images: dryness, darkness, the inner 'desert' when all is bleak and nothing seems to be happening in prayer. Accept this state, she exhorts; do not shun it, but keep on acknowledging God's love through the aridity.

The way of daily prayer and contemplation is not an easy one for Georges, either. He cannot confide in a spiritual director with his wife's openness, but eventually he, like her, will find a way through the frustration of dryness and distraction. The married life of Pauline and Georges Vanier will become, in its own way, an act of oblation to God's merciful love, and certainly the heart of St Thérèse's act will beat in the whole of their lives and in their desire to do everything for God. For Pauline's part, Mother Mary of the Cross has a deep understanding of her needs, and she cautions Pauline against extraordinary practices, such as depriving herself of what is necessary in fulfilling her obligations. In fact, in response to Pauline who accuses herself of being self-indulgent when others are suffering, the prioress reminds her sternly of her 'positive duty' in her diplomatic role. The sacrifices required of Pauline are already real enough.

As the years go on, Pauline and Georges will deepen their relationship with God and with each other, and like St Thérèse, they are living more and more deeply at the heart of the Church. During the post-war years, the couple will find spiritual support at the Carmel of Nogent-sur-Marne, a short drive from Paris. Pauline will become a Carmelite tertiary there. The couple will embrace prayer and service in the way that Carmelites through the centuries have chosen: the way of simplicity, trusting in God's loving mercy, acknowledging their own weakness, and echoing St Thérèse as they say with St Paul, 'When I am weak, then I am strong.' [13]

Along the way, they will meet a Dominican priest, Thomas Philippe. He will become a guide for Pauline, helping her to deepen her understanding of God's merciful love. The Vanier children will gradually move into adulthood following spiritual paths that Pauline, without realizing it, has opened for them. The oldest son becomes a Trappist monk named Benedict. He will be ordained a priest two weeks before Mother Mary of the Cross's death in 1952 and will be regarded by his parents as the family's spiritual rock.

Seven years later, Georges Vanier will be elevated to prominence as the Governor General of Canada. His fellow Canadians will come to recognize the inner strength that lies beneath his wise words and friendly simplicity. They will note the patience with which he bears his increasing infirmity. Only after his death will they discover the rich sources of his spiritual life.

During Georges Vanier's time in office, son Jean, with Père Thomas, will found a new small community which they call 'L'Arche'. Georges Vanier, the mainstay of Pauline's life, will die in 1967, and as a widow, Pauline will find a new vocation. She will be educated in what she calls 'the school of L'Arche'. As she moves into advanced old age she will rely increasingly on her son Benedict whose gentle transatlantic messages will echo, in the language of a new generation, the spiritual counsel of the Carmelite prioress. St Thérèse writes in her Act of Oblation, 'In the evening of this life I shall appear before You with empty hands'. [14] For Pauline, it is a lifetime's courageous struggle to hold her hands open in trust.

St Thérèse found in Paul's first letter to the Corinthians a signpost on her little way. Likewise, Georges and

Pauline Vanier, both singly and together, strive to live out Paul's injunction, 'Now you are the body of Christ'. [15] As they navigate their own path through their own particular time and place, they can remind themselves at every step, 'Now you have received mercy'. [16]

ONE

The Door of the Heart 1938-1942

'By exercising their proper function and being
led by the spirit of the gospel they can work
for the sanctification of the world from within,
in the manner of leaven. In this way they can
make Christ known to others, especially by the
testimony of a life resplendent in faith, hope and
charity.'
Dogmatic Constitution of the Church, Chapter IV
'The Laity' #31

Although Georges and Pauline Vanier were both from
Montreal, by the spring of 1938 they had spent ten of
their seventeen years of marriage in Europe.

Georges Vanier turned fifty in 1938. He was a law-
yer by training, a wounded veteran of World War I,
and after the war he had become the commander of
Canada's francophone regiment, known as the Royal
22nd Regiment. His posting as a military advisor at the
League of Nations in Geneva had led to a diplomatic
career, and he had been sent as second in authority to
the Canadian High Commission in London in 1931.
Temperamentally he was reserved, highly disciplined,

exacting and idealistic, with a dry sense of humour and a penchant for English nineteenth-century poetry.

He had been brought up in the atmosphere of a heavily Jansenistic Catholicism, and as a result his practice of the faith was governed by a rigid fear of God's punishment and an exaggerated sense of unworthiness. He received Communion only once or twice a year, and then only if he had been to Confession immediately beforehand lest he be in a state of sin a few minutes later. (He had made a retreat as a young man to determine whether he had a vocation to the priesthood. Among his thirteen retreat resolutions: 'To keep guard on myself for the sin of sloth and...to make a note of the times I am idle and to think, at least once a day, of the number of times I have been slothful and to examine the causes of it' and 'To think once a day of Hell and its torments'.)

Pauline, ten years his junior, was his exact opposite in temperament and outlook. As the only child of a Quebec Superior Court judge, she lived within a well-to-do milieu. Although she was intelligent and learned easily, her schooling had been conducted mainly by a succession of governesses of limited ability. Her extroversion and spontaneity went hand-in-hand with a streak of anxiety and a tendency to slip into depression. But from her mother she had imbibed a spirit of trust in God's love. In later years she would speak of Georges's shock at the idea that, as a daily communicant, she could drink champagne and dance all night, and then receive communion the next morning without any feeling of guilt.

In early 1928 the Vaniers moved to Geneva, where Georges became Canada's military representative to the League of Nations. By this time, the strain of motherhood to three children (Thérèse, Georges – nicknamed 'Byngsie' after his honourary godfather, Lord Byng – and Bernard), as well as the expectation of diplomatic entertaining, had taken its toll on Pauline. Pregnant with her fourth child in the spring of 1928, she was threatened with a miscarriage. After the child, named Jean (and given the nickname 'Jock'), was delivered safely that September, she suffered an emotional breakdown and was hospitalized.

The stock market crash followed the next year, and shortly afterward Georges was named First Secretary to the Canadian High Commission in London. The Vaniers found themselves in a diplomatic milieu where they were expected to keep up appearances without sufficient means. By the mid-1930s, with the family's finances back on an even keel, Pauline began to feel healthy again. To help her move out of herself, her doctor suggested that she visit young miners who were dying of lung disease. In doing this, she added a dimension to her life that, in one way or another, would continue for the rest of her life.

At this time Pauline also felt the need to pursue spiritual help. This she found at the Jesuit church on Farm Street in London, where she met a Jesuit in his mid-sixties by the name of Roger Clutton, who was in poor health and had deteriorating eyesight. He was known to be a spiritual director of gentleness and kindness and was described after his death as 'one whose strength was made perfect in infirmity'. [17] She began receiving spiritual counselling from Father Clutton.

Pauline also began to attend a series of talks known as Wednesday Conferences, given by another Jesuit, Robert Steuart, who was one of England's best known preachers at the time. Father Steuart had come through his own periods of suffering. His family belonged to the landed gentry of Scotland, and his youth had been one of indolence and lavish living. As a young Jesuit he continually castigated himself for being lazy, self-centred and vain. He had bouts of depression and struggles with his prayer life, and eventually in frustration he sought help in prayer from the prioress of the Notting Hill Carmel. From his own experience, he spoke of prayer as not so much following a rote formula, but rather of presenting oneself before God, with an act of faith that it is God who takes the initiative in prayer. He exhorted his listeners to accept dryness, depression, and feelings of alienation just as they are and not as obstacles to prayer. Pauline became a devotee of Father Steuart and his Wednesday Conferences.

On Good Friday, April 15, 1938, Father Steuart was scheduled to preach at St Ignatius Church in the London borough of Hackney. Reluctantly – perhaps having heard his wife enthuse over this priest once too often – Georges agreed to accompany her to the service. The Good Friday afternoon service of the 1930s, known as

'Devotions of the Three Hours' Agony', consisted of a sermon on the last words of Jesus on the Cross. Father Steuart was known to speak energetically on the love of God, often using down to earth language and gentle humour ('Some people seem to think of God as if He were in a chronic state of irritation with them'[18]). He himself also was said to be especially drawn to the Passion as the entry to God's love ('What was the last appearance of Christ before He died? On the Cross with His Arms stretched out as if He would say, "Such has been My Love for you; nailed, so that I cannot withdraw if I would"[19]). Whatever were his specific words in that sermon on Good Friday 1938, when Georges Vanier heard them, they marked an important spiritual turning point for him, having the effect of finally opening the door of moral and spiritual rigidity that had gradually become unlocked during his seventeen-year marriage to Pauline.

In August of that year, in her annual letter commemorating the anniversary of Georges's wounding in battle, Pauline wrote, 'If I've always admired and loved you tenderly, never before this year have I felt such communion of soul and heart with you.' Georges replied, 'Yes, *mon cheri*, this year there is something new, more beautiful and greater in our love. This change is due to you, to your example, to your prayers, and I thank you for it with all my heart.'[20] Not long afterward, he began to accompany Pauline to daily Mass and Communion, and at some point during the turbulent years that followed, they decided to spend an additional half an hour each day in prayer.

Toward the end of 1938 Georges Vanier learned that he had been appointed head of the Canadian legation in France. In a speech at the Savoy Hotel, he paid tribute to Pauline: 'I owe much to her inspiration, much to her advice and criticism in which for my good she is not always sparing. Without her by my side, I would not like to face the task in Paris.' [21] His tone was lighthearted, but the message was real: he was aware of how much he owed to his wife.

As for Pauline herself, another door had opened up for her. The Jesuit Father Clutton was a friend of the Carmelite monastery in the town of Hitchin in Hertfordshire, a short train ride from London. He recommended to Pauline that she visit the prioress there. The prioress's name was Mother Mary of the Cross. She was only seven years older than Pauline, but she carried the wisdom of a woman much older. She had been born in Ireland and had known tragedy at a young age, having lost two brothers in infancy, followed by the lengthy illness and death of her mother and the death of another brother in World War I. She had been named prioress at the relatively young age of 34. For the rest of her life Mother Mary of the Cross would provide a spiritual lifeline for Pauline Vanier.

Georges and Pauline prepared to move to Paris in early 1939 amid a shaky uncertainty throughout Europe. For herself, Pauline was not so sure about the move into the unknown, with none of her usual supports. Early in the new year of 1939, Mother Mary of the Cross wrote:

> I write to say 'Courage. Sursum corda [Lift up your hearts].' Keep your eyes on Him and be His very little Child so that in all He may hold and guide you....
>
> ...He wants *peace* in your soul, my Pauline – He works in peace. And He must be free in you to work the plan of His Love. 'A Child is born to us'. And He wants to take new birth in your soul, to use just *you* to live again His Life before His Father and so to use you to radiate Himself into His Mystical Body, the Church.
>
> Make your weakness your very pleading to Him, that He may give His Love to you all the more. 'Miseri-cor-dare' – to give the heart to a wretched one is just the meaning of mercy. So weary not to remind Him how much you need Him.
>
> Every struggle has its blows, its falls, its hours of utter weariness. But with Him all is easy. By faith and love let Him live more and more within you, in unshakeable confidence. He knocks at the door of your heart – open wide to Him & let Him come in, and hold Him fast in joy and confidence, and so let Him find rest in your soul.

Here I am, holding you in my prayer. *He* is waiting for you in Paris so fear not – but make the move in peace and surrender to His Blessed Will. Accept it. Will it.

Father Clutton wrote as well:

….Be assured you are all right. God has a hold on you and you would have to push Him off if you would be free from Him – which please God you will not do.

Be faithful to prayer and realise that you must depend on Him for all things. You cannot do without Him. Pray in the way you find easiest. You say it is easy now, but it won't always be so. The sun is shining but it won't always be fine weather.

You are in a rush of social duties etc. Try always to take God with you. Remember He is there in you even if lunching or at dinner or a reception. But you must fulfil your social duties to the best of your power. Don't mind your vanities – laugh at yourself.

I am glad you have found a confessor. I hope he won't try to lace you up too tightly. Be cautious what you say about your prayers. Many good priests do not understand. You could always say, if he is too inquisitive, you have a director in England. I expect you will be over before too long and you can have a full talk….'[22]

In Paris, the Vanier couple continued to be daily communicants, and for their daily half hour of prayer and meditation they discovered the tranquil Blessed Sacrament Chapel, which was tucked into a narrow street of townhouses called rue Cortambert. The chapel was open day and night, and it was possible to slip inside at any time, leaving the busy sounds of the nearby Place du Trocadéro.

They had decided that their four children would spend the remainder of the school year at their boarding schools in England – sixteen-year-old Thérèse at Mayfield in Sussex, fourteen-year old Byngsie, and the two youngest, Bernard and Jean, twelve and eleven, at St John's Beaumont, near Windsor. In June, 1939, the rector of St John's informed them by phone that Byngsie had taken dangerously ill as a result of a burst appendix. A serious infection threatened his life. His parents rushed across the English Channel to his side and sat by helplessly until it eventually became clear that the crisis was over. In later years Pauline would recall the days of anguish when Byngsie's life hung in the balance. As she wept, the Jesuit rector told her she must accept the will of God regarding the boy. She would remember that in response she stammered a 'dead or alive' offering of her son to God.

The Vaniers returned to an increasingly fraught Paris, where extra trains were mobilized for evacuations. The atmosphere was tense as everyone waited to see what the next international move would be. In August, Pauline, her mother and the four children went for their annual holiday to the seaside town of Varenge-ville, on the Normandy coast, where they would be safe if bombs were aimed at Paris or London.

They were still at the seaside when Germany invaded Poland on 1 September. Britain and France declared war the next day. Canada's declaration of war followed a week later. It was decided that the family would stay together for the time being, and they found rental rooms in a section of an old chateau in the countryside, while Georges remained at the legation in Paris.

For Pauline, it was a time of intolerable waiting, in an unfamiliar place amid tension and fear, close to where war had been declared. Her anxiety flared as day after day there was no telling what lay ahead of them. Mother Mary of the Cross wrote on 21 September:

> I am so sorry to hear that you are in the Desert …
> or rather I should not say 'sorry' for I know Our
> Beloved Lord is by this means preparing your soul
> for closer union and asking you for a deeper sur-
> render of your will.
>
> Turn to the Blessed Trinity within and just get
> fresh strength in the sanctuary of your soul. Unite
> your suffering with Our Lord's in every Mass at
> which you are Priest and Victim with Him – so
> that He can use you as a life in which He con-
> tinues to adore His Father.
>
> It is your present cross, Child, to bear this dark-
> ness – but Our Holy Father St John of the Cross
> speaks so wonderfully of carrying our cross with

Him as the means of sanctity (*Ascent*, Book II Chap 6 & 7).

All your sisters join me in sending their love. We often speak of you.

I must end with a big blessing and devoted love.

News began filtering through about the amassing of troops and atrocities committed in Poland against Jews and people of Slavic origin. Pauline spent day after day in distress, her fragile temperament near the breaking point. On 4 December, the prioress wrote,

> Your dear letter was a great pleasure to me, and though Our Beloved Lord is leading you by a 'tractless waterless' way with dull grey clouds about, yet He has one only purpose as you say, to secure your will for Himself alone and to have the mouth of your desires open towards Him in all.
>
> Smile to Him at His strange way of loving – and give Him that WILL more & more & more, my Pauline, with joy. '*Gaudete in Domino et Verum dico vobis gaudete.*' ['Rejoice in the Lord, and truly I say rejoice.']
>
> Yes, you are ever in my prayer and love – and I am happy that this can bring comfort to you.

By the beginning of 1940 nothing had changed in the Vaniers' circumstances, and it was unclear what their own next move should be – either to move back to Paris or to return to Canada. Domestic tension increased.

Although the three Vanier boys attended the local
school, they became restless, with little outlet for their
boisterous energy. The strain of their living conditions
wore on Pauline's nerves, and it was a small relief for
her to escape the oppressiveness of their situation by
spending a few days with Georges in Paris. She wrote
of her irritability and her spiritual darkness to Mother
Mary of the Cross. The prioress replied on 26 January:

> I am so glad Georges has you with him a bit. But
> what an anxiety about the boys....
>
> Your spiritual life is *right* – despite a zero tem-
> perature. Yes – the ever tranquil Trinity dwells
> within & even when we are not conscious of it, it
> is there, a fact of God's outpouring love to help &
> balance us.
>
> The irritability is a big trial. But that is mainly
> physical. Your life has been a big strain in so many
> ways since June. The best use we can make of it
> (those of us who suffer from it – hush! hush!) is
> to humble ourselves very entirely before God and
> thank Him for forcing us to see our misery and
> nothingness and our joyous need of *Him*....
>
> All join in sending much, much love and ever
> our loving prayer. They all love you too. And my
> Pauline, yes, I think I know a little what God in
> His Love has put in your heart for me – bless you.
> I am so happy to have it.

In April of 1940, with matters in France still seem-
ingly at a standstill, the Vanier family, along with others, moved back to Paris, tentatively optimistic that life
might return to normal. On 11 May the German army
charged into Belgium, and then Holland. By the end of
May, the tanks had reached France's borders. A quick
decision was now needed. While Georges remained
in Paris to close the Canadian legation, Pauline, her
mother and children left in a legation car for the port of
Bordeaux, on a road filled with cars, carts, bicycles, and
people on foot, all desperate to flee the coming enemy.
After several months during which nothing seemed to
be happening, events were taking place so quickly during these days that it is a wonder that the prioress's
next letter, written 14 May, reached Pauline.

> My dearest Child,
>
> A word of love and instant prayer in this big
> crisis both for you in France and in your own little
> family circle.
>
> Is Byngsie better again?
>
> The news is staggering but much as I feared it
> would come about.
>
> We can only one and all trust in God's actual
> grace to meet each crisis as it comes with calm &
> determination.
>
> May Our Lady hold you very close, my Pauline.

At the coastal village of Le Verdon-sur-Mer a British
destroyer picked up the family, along with a handful

of others, and they steamed into the Bay of Biscay, manoeuvring around German U-boats as explosions sounded in the distance. The boat at last reached Milford Haven in Wales, and the exhausted family went on to London, waiting for news of Georges's whereabouts. Mother Mary of the Cross wrote on 23 June:

> Only prayer can be the comfort I offer, for words just fail in this flood of anguish and grief and pain.
>
> You must be exhausted and weary in soul and mind and heart and body....
>
> I would love to have you for a few days in the Lodge – is it possible? You must just keep as silent about it as possible. But come if you can. I know it is hard to get here and that you may have duties but I think it would do you good.
>
> I will wait to have a line – and to know if you have word of Georges.
>
> My big enfolding love – I trust you to Our Lady's care....

Pauline remained frantic with worry about Georges's safety until he arrived in London a few days later, having escaped from France on a sardine boat. The Vanier children and Pauline's mother left almost immediately by ship for Montreal. Georges and Pauline were recalled back to Canada by the Canadian government the following September.

In Hitchin, daily life had become increasingly deprived for the Carmelites as the war raged. They lost

a portion of their income through the loss of a bene-
factor. As part of their war effort, they gave some of
their garden produce to the navy. When the German
bombing raids began in the autumn of 1940, younger
nuns were occupied in all-night fire squads, and air raid
alerts threatened the monastery's daily routine. Prayer
begun in the chapel was sometimes completed in the
cellar. 'The spirit here is great – no flinching – "grim
and gay" is a real description of it,' Mother Mary of the
Cross wrote to Pauline in an undated letter. And in
another, indicating the new state of things, 'Let us keep
our souls in His Peace, amid life's variations. We had an
incendiary bomb in the Lane last week.'

The Vaniers gave the Carmelites a cow, and the milk
helped to make up for the general food shortage. They
also kept goats and chickens at the monastery, and with
money donated by the Vaniers, they followed the general advice to British citizens to lay in a small stock of
food as provision 'in case of invasion'.

In Canada, the Vaniers settled into their new war-
time reality. Thérèse, who had finished school, took a
secretarial course, and the three boys enrolled in Loyola
College in Montreal. Georges Vanier was sent to per-
suade people in the heavily French province of Quebec
to support Canada's war effort and to recruit volun-
teers for the army. He and Pauline were shocked to find
that in Quebec there was indifference to the bombing
of Britain and, in many places, outright support for the
return to 'traditional values' of Marshal Pétain's pup-
pet government in Vichy. Pauline gave talks to Quebec

women about their harrowing escape from France and the terrifying experiences of the French people.

Amid the upheaval of the family's life, Pauline discovered in the late autumn of 1940 that at the age of 42 she was once again pregnant. She wrote to Mother Mary of the Cross about her 'shock' and her spirit's 'numbness' and the worry that always faced her: that she failed as a mother.

On 21 February 1941 the Carmelite prioress replied:

> And now for the big and holy and happy secret. Just Magnificat together. Indeed I realise in some little manner the shock: and the difficulty it must have seemed. But it is surely not only a grace from God but a special grace and trust. May Our Lady be very near you all the time and her own loved Mother, St Anne, caring and guiding you in all. Let me know how you are in health from time to time. I have told just the ones you knew best here, and you know it will go no further....
>
> Raids have not been so bad....Of course the London fire raid was terrible and the ghastly attacks on Coventry etc. But the spirit of the people is more amazing than one could say – it really takes seeing to believe it. Just ordinary folk, bombed out 3 & 4 times, making far less fuss than they might have done if the milkman had not delivered their morning milk!
>
> ....Pauline, child – accept to be numb at Mass and even at Holy Communion. Mass is Calvary

– numbness, pain, agony – so suffer with Him, giving Him the ready union of your will with His own will in this supreme act of loving adoration of His Father which He perpetuates in His Priest, and in *you* through your royal priesthood. I am sure, sure, sure He is pleased with you. Keep more & more in His Peace. And let not your failures trouble you. Your children are ever sure of your loving goodness to them. And He is waiting, as the most loving Mother.

I love Dame Juliana's setting out of Our Lord as our Mother (in 'The Revelations of Divine Love') – 'God Almighty is our kindly Father; and God, All-Wisdom is our kindly Mother; with the love and the goodness of the Holy Ghost: which is all one God, one Lord'.....

In the early spring, fourteen-year-old Bernard was taken ill with rheumatic fever and spent several weeks in hospital. After Pauline wrote that the worst of the illness was over, but that she still worried about her unborn baby and her own maternal failings, Mother Mary of the Cross wrote:

How comforting for you to have him better. I have had rheumatic fever, so I know its horrors. Yes, take every wise precaution over the heart. I had 'compensation' for the valve affected, so it left no serious result.

Pauline dearest, the little one on its way is truly God's gift to you – and both you & Georges will remain young for many extra years. You have our prayer indeed and I like to feel that you can say that you are serene. You must be very busy....

Someone has, I believe, summed up the Hess affair[23] in the following:

1. 'It is the mell of a Hess.'
2. 'Hess's opinion of Hitler
   Has clearly grown littler
   While Hitler's opinion of Hess
   Is probably less.'

Pauline, the people here are *amazing.* The spirit beyond understanding. A surgical instrument maker spoke to me the other day of being three times bombed out, in the way he might say he had three times lost a bus ticket. They just go on, however bad it is. And it has been pretty bad. Though in the West End there is not really much to see. Sr. Josephine was up in town last week for the first time since the blitz, and though she was all 'round the Oxford Street and Strand part, she was astonished that, save on the actual spots where bombs and mines had fallen, everything looked so ordinary.

Poor God – amidst it all, what peace to know He loves us all the time and even when His children fight, that we humans are His children still. And how a childlike spirit in us must rest Him. One can almost see His point of view about St Teresa of the Child Jesus. She certainly had simplicity of intention – the single eye for God that sounds so easy but is really in itself a loving practice of all the virtues. Do you know the Holy Father's wonderful sermon at the Mass of her canonization? [24] If not, do read it, but read it slowly and prayerfully. I had, about 6 years ago, felt very specially drawn to her and his words came as a confirmation of that drawing.

Michel Paul Vanier was born in Quebec City on 29 July 1941. No sooner had he arrived in the world than two other Vanier children were making moves to leave the safety of Canada and cross the Atlantic. Thérèse, turned nineteen in February 1942, and having completed her secretarial course, decided to join the Mechanized Transport Corps, which was recruiting young Canadian women to become motor mechanics and drivers for the armed forces in England.

At the same time, the Vaniers' third son, Jean, barely thirteen years old, asked his father's permission to continue his schooling at the Royal Naval College in Dartmouth, England. The prospect of sending her children – especially young Jean – across the deadly Atlantic, horrified Pauline. The Carmelite prioress commiserated with her grief at the leave-taking prospect, and exhorted her in an undated letter, 'Do not bother as to what is coming – live with Him in the *present* – give

all and rejoice.' Pauline may have needed above all the
blessing expressed by the prioress in a further letter:
'May Our Lady wrap you round for me – and remember, the humdrum of life lived with her for Him is the
ALL He asks.' Of all the partings in Pauline's life up to
now, letting Jean go at such a young age may have been
the hardest.

In the autumn of 1942 Georges received the news
that he was to be named the Canadian Minister to the
Governments in Exile in London. This meant that
another upheaval was in store for the Vanier family. In the meantime, after Michel's birth, Pauline had
resumed speeches in aid of the war effort to Quebec's
women's groups. The prioress wrote for Christmas:

> Now He must joy [sic] to know that you are ready
> and happy to sit at His feet and wait – your will in
> His: a real secret of holiness. Yes: I am sure it is
> Our Lord loving His Father, through us, using us
> still to love Him.
>
> My Pauline dearest, the lack of prayer seems
> terrible, the lack of understanding of the need.
> Bravo! Do talk about it, placed as you are, I mean:
> 1. By your own attractive personality, 2. By your
> own social position you can reap a rich harvest for
> God by your nice insistence on this point of pray-
> er. And do it when you get to England too. And
> I hope you will be ready quietly to continue your
> public speaking here – you are the right type. Oh

the criticism matters not at all, as you say. I was so very pleased to know that you were doing all this.

As Georges was all set to leave for London, he took sick and was hospitalized with pneumonia. Christmas of 1942 was bleak because the family was so scattered, and in a note to his two oldest sons, Georges exhorted them to 'look after your Mummy and be thoughtful with her during these holy days,' [25] noting that their family was at least intact, unlike some others that the war had touched.

But by the early spring of 1943 he would be recovered and Pauline would find her family once again geographically splintered.

TWO

Weakness Calling Forth Mercy: 1943 - 44

'The deeper one is drawn into God, the more one
must go 'out of oneself'; that is, one must go to
the world in order to carry the divine life in it.'
*Edith Stein: Self-Portrait in
Letters*, letter to a friend

When Georges Vanier accepted the post of Canadian
Representative to the Governments in Exile in 1943,
he knew that Pauline's help was essential. Echoing her
pre-wedding letter to him twenty-two years earlier, he
wrote to her: 'As in the past, I want our destiny to be
together, not only in thought but also in daily action.'
[26] After her husband's departure for England in March
1943, Pauline was left with the decision to break up
the family further by leaving Canada and joining him.
It was a choice that would haunt her for the rest of her
life. She felt that the two older boys in Montreal, now
teenagers, could manage without her, but it was the
youngest, Michel, not yet two years old, who needed
her. In the end, her seventy-year-old mother, Thérèse
de Salaberry Archer, readily agreed to look after the
child with the help of a nanny.

Pauline boarded a plane for London on 21 June. She was reunited with her husband and also, for a short while, after a year's separation, with Thérèse and Jean. It was the start of a new aspect of her vocation, and Mother Mary of the Cross wrote to her on 4 July:

> I hope you will find really good soul help. Yes, I love to think of you and Georges with daily Mass and Our Lord sanctifying the Kingdom of your soul and acting within you in His daily visit: making you more and more like Himself.
>
> I think your inability to 'stay put' while you were waiting to come over was indeed beyond your control and rose from an unavoidable nervous tension.
>
> But now that you are safely here, be faithful to that prayer as much as you can. God is asking you for that, and mainly counting on you to give Him thus a special glory by your faithful love and to help souls in that way.
>
> Of course at times your very 'duties of your state of life' may and will prevent it, but let us join our prayer, Pauline dearest.

In August she managed to spend time at the Hitchin Carmel, and she found the nuns using every piece of the monastery's grounds to grow as much produce as possible. Hens and goats had joined the Vaniers' gift of a cow in helping to make the monastery nearly self-supporting. The Carmelites had recently had elections,

and Mother Mary of the Cross was no longer the prioress. Although she found it a 'real grace' to be out of
office, it was also 'not entirely easy after 18 years....'

As for Pauline, for the past four years her life had
consisted of one upheaval after another. And now, in
the midst of bombed London, which was still in a state
of emergency, where many were homeless, and where
she had hoped to help with relief work, her role consisted in visiting displaced royalty and diplomats who
were living in relative luxury. In letters to her mother and older sons, she wondered whether it had been
worth her while in leaving her small child in the care of
others, while also dealing from afar with the domestic
issues that her mother wrote about regularly. Given
these circumstances, there was little in prayer to comfort her. After her return to London from her time at
the Hitchin Carmel, Mother Mary of the Cross wrote
on 26 August:

> It was great great joy to have you – and a real soul
> comfort to feel that God is drawing you so lovingly
> all the time (He draws most in darkness) and that
> your love is reaching out to Him in your willed
> surrender. Give Him this always, no matter how
> you feel. Feelings are a great nuisance but they do
> not really matter much. What are you to do, my
> Pauline. I can only say – give Him your *love*, give
> Him your *desires*. I give you my full assurance that
> it is all very much right. Those desires do come
> from God.

As you say, they may go right away for a long period, and then come back in force. But that makes no difference. I repeat & repeat again – they *are* of God. God told St Catherine of Siena that He would be served in an infinite manner & she had nothing infinite about her save her desires.

Keep your soul in peace – God works in peace, the devil in noise & turmoil. And remember we are so like clocks, we just run out & need to be wound up again. So inflame those desires from time to time – always in deepening peace.

Indeed there is no delusion. But even if there were, you would accept a decision that it was delusion, so do have no anxiety.

God is, as I see it, drawing you close. Pray – direct prayer – as regularly as you can & trust it to Him when you cannot. Be a little child with Him in all and just open wide to give Him your heart.

Pauline remained lonely for Michel ('how I wish I could hold him … and hear his first words, which are now probably becoming sentences') and wept over snapshots of her toddler son that her mother sent her. She zig-zagged between wondering if she had made the wrong decision in joining her husband – if in doing so she was going against God's will for her – and trying to console herself by regarding her decision as the choice of a greater good ('the sacrifice is so small compared with the sufferings of so many others'). [27] And in the midst of the whirlwind of her life, she found little time for her usual half hour of prayer.

At Farm Street church, she discovered that her old spiritual director, Father Clutton, had moved out of London, but Father Steuart, whose Good Friday sermon before the war had meant so much to the couple, agreed to see her. She wrote to her mother, 'He greeted me with real affection and kept me for three quarters of an hour. What a saint. He clarified in a precise way certain matters that have been worrying me ... Father Steuart renewed in me a feeling of calm that I badly needed ... He told me to continue my life in the world and not to worry about not being able to make my prayer visit, but even to accept it ... Father Steuart is so right in telling me that my duty is to be a woman in the world and to try as much as possible to radiate His love around me.'[28]

Sustained by Father Steuart's affirmation, Pauline found herself once again in a state of consolation, and wrote to Mother Mary of the Cross in this frame of mind – and then wondered why God was treating her with such special attention. The Carmelite responded on 8 September:

> ....on Monday came your dear letter with such happy word of the graces God is giving to your soul. Take what it offers in great peace and joy, and when time lacks, to give Him *direct* prayer, just make the duties of your state of life, done for Him direct, the happy messengers of your love.

Have no worry about any unresponsiveness there may seem to be, my Pauline. God is acting in a supernatural way & often His actions rouse no response in our weak human nature. When it is like that, just accept it – bear your creaturehood, one might say – & in fact thank Him that it is from His loving Hands you came.

Indeed, we can say 'Why me...' and the answer is a very simple little one, not because I am good but because He *is goodness*. Our beloved Holy Mother puts it for us: 'His Majesty loves to show His power in frail souls because in them His goodness meets with the least obstacle' (I cannot look up the exact words at this moment, but that is what she expresses).

You say you are totally unworthy of Him. My Pauline, each touch He gives of Himself shows that to our soul more & more clearly. And He wills it so. He wants us to love our dependence on Him. His own words...He 'the Father'...me 'the little child'.

In the same letter Mother Mary of the Cross broached the suggestion that Pauline become a Third Order Carmelite, thus living the contemplative way of life of Carmel outside the cloister, in her own sphere of life. 'I think we should go slowly in the decision, lest obligations, slight though they are, might be a burden,' she wrote. There is no indication of how Pauline reacted to this new suggestion. In the meantime, she lunched with kings and dined with princes, and meanwhile, on the war front, the news was promising. After the retreat of the German army from Russia several months earlier, the news came through that the Allies had successfully invaded Italy. General de Gaulle had arrived in Algiers to establish his provisional French government. And in early October, Georges was appointed the Canadian representative to de Gaulle's government and thus was soon to depart for Algiers.

Pauline, who, with the help of the Carmelite and the Jesuit close at hand, had just become reconciled to the role of a socialite she did not want to play, now faced a separation from her husband. Mother Mary of the Cross responded to the news on 22 October:

> God's loving goodness to your soul was just preparing you for this fresh surrender. He seems to me, in His own way, to be asking you for very complete and entire self-abnegation & detachment that He may work in you His will and good pleasure.
>
> Dryness nearly always follows a big grace-e.g. the holiest Profession retreat will probably have the heaviest re-action. So have no fear. Just love Him – and rest in Him – and give Him your will.... Christ, the King *there*, in very truth, must you & I make Him each in our different 'state' of life....
>
> It is grief to feel you are going, were not one sure that it is God's direct working for your soul and your perfection.

Later that autumn, before Georges's leave-taking, the
Carmelite informed Pauline that she and the Mother
Prioress would be visiting London for the prioress to
see an oculist on Wimpole Street. She asked whether
they might lunch at Pauline and Georges's small flat.
The visit took place after a flurry of letters back and
forth, and the Carmelite wrote to thank her on 9 November:

> It was great joy to be with you in your own home
> and a great comfort to me to feel how God's Love
> has drawn us together and was our first bond.
> Thank you for all you did for us, all so sweetly
> done and with so much love.
>
> And oh my Pauline, give Him just that loving
> turning to Him that He asks so that He may ever
> take great pleasure in your soul – in your home
> and in the life of each one. Do let us together, let
> our turning be towards Him asking Our Lady to
> hold us …
>
> I am sure your penance is joyful humility in
> your failures to give the little acts He seems to ask
> as tokens of your deliberate loving choice of Him
> – rather than any repining about your weakness.
> That weakness calls forth His mercy – 'Miseri-cor-
> dare'- to give His Heart to a wretched one, is it
> not? So our very misery draws Him.
>
> We thought of King Haakon [of Norway] and
> 'Their Excellencies' and I asked God's blessing on

your meeting and on Georges's happy task to help
to build up peace.

Georges's plane bound for Algiers took off at the end
of December, as Pauline, Thérèse and Jean waved him
away. In an undated note, Mother Mary of the Cross
wrote, 'Only a brief note to bring loving prayer in the
separation which Our Lord is asking of you. But you
and Georges are working for God's kingdom. So take
all sweetly and direct from Him.' She added, 'I consider [Georges's] work as utterly for God as any work
could be – helping to direct aright our European rela-
tions with country and country.'

Early in the new year of 1944 Pauline learned that
she was shortly to join Georges in Algiers. This prospect brought a new set of anxieties: the plane journey,
the departure from her two children in England, the
alien destination. She made a visit to the Hitchin Carmel before departing. On 2 February, Mother Mary of
the Cross wrote:

> I am with you in thought more and more these
> days and trusting Him with you and for you.
>
> Keep your will in His – and if in the pressure &
> strain of getting off, prayer is cold & you are weary
> – never mind. Keep peace. And just be a living
> hearth of His Love.
>
> Write when you can and know how much we
> are with you, holding you and Georges before
> Him every moment; and the dear, dear children....

May our sweet Mother watch over you and
make your life fruitful for Her Son in its simple
fidelity and joy in the various duties of your state.

Pauline left England and joined her husband in Algiers
just before Lent, having wondered aloud to Mother
Mary of the Cross during her visit what she would do
for a Lenten penance. On 23 February, after Pauline's
arrival in Algiers, the Carmelite wrote, 'You will be having very real Lenten penances, if rather unusual ones –
separation, cutting off, etc. Be in His Hand – love Him.
And give Him a resting place in your soul, even when
fixed prayer seems not possible. Above all and over all,
keep in His Peace.'

In Algiers Pauline found two groups of people: diplomats, generals, European and American officials of various kinds; and, closer to the city's core, Arabs who were
mostly living in filth and squalor. Her initial impression
of Arabs, so exotic and foreign to her, was a negative
one: they were dirty, shifty, not to be trusted. In the
countryside she formed another impression of Algeria's
native population. She wrote to her son Byngsie, 'Some
of them are really magnificent, quite biblical in appearance, especially those who wear the long hooded brown
cloaks and [walk] barefooted. You meet them on the
country roads tending sheep or goats.' And again, on
one occasion, as they passed some Arab men: 'they
looked at us with a certain scorn, a look which seemed
to mean, "You may think that you're grand because you
drive about in cars, but we are the people that really

belong here, not you!'" She added, 'How they must hate the whites who have installed themselves in these lands, using them more or less as slaves - to do what? Make money!' [29]

To her dismay, Pauline found her main duty was seeing to domestic affairs – keeping a cook employed, and at times doing the cooking herself, making the makeshift household run smoothly so that generals and ambassadors could be entertained. The Vaniers were housed in a villa outside of Algiers that looked like a film set and overlooked the Mediterranean, but the interior of the building was Spartan rather than grand. She wrote to her son Jean about feeling useless and wished to do something useful: 'there are times when I would like to chuck it all overboard and go to work in one of the hospitals where they are in need of help, but I suppose that wouldn't be doing my duty.' [30]

By late spring the Vaniers were already hearing horrendous stories about Gestapo arrests and terrorism taking place in Europe, and were receiving visits from former prisoners of war and members of the French Resistance who slipped over to Algiers to meet with de Gaulle. Tension increased throughout the spring as the planned Allied D-Day landing approached. She continued to monitor young Michel's progress at a distance and at least once during her stay in Algiers she considered returning to Montreal. Her general feeling of uselessness continued as she entertained field marshals and generals, drinking fine Algerian wine and smoking cigarettes, aware that a short distance across the sea others were suffering torment. And yet, in some sense she knew her present state was what God wanted for her.

On 4 June Mother Mary of the Cross wrote:

> Your letter of May 20th delights me. And I take full responsibility in telling you that it *is* God's drawing and to go fearlessly & humbly perseveringly along the path indicated – *prayer* and a prayer life even amid your many calls & seemingly conflicting duties. Why should not God have souls to serve Him in that way, just *because* of & *in spite* of circumstances so strange.
>
> I enjoyed the story of the cigarette while you were writing, almost as much as if I had smoked it!
>
> That is just *us*; a mass of contradictions and strange conflicting draws. Now for God, now for self. But He is so tender. He knows our weakness so well and *He* bears with us. So we must just bear with ourselves, acknowledging our creaturehood and humbling ourselves before Him in our own hearts when we fail. Our failures are part of the game, part of the 'fun' I nearly said! Because in them we learn our real weakness, our nothingness. And this nothingness *acknowledged* and yes, even loved, is the right & best material for His Mercy – *miseri-cor-dia*, i.e. *miseri* – to the wretched one; *cor* – my heart – *do* – I give.
>
> He calls us to prayer not because *we* are good, but because He is good and longs to share that

goodness in close union with His little creature. In prayer comes strength. 'Quia Tua es Deus, fortitude mea.' ['For you are God, my strength.'] In prayer, we leave Him free to be our own Holiness. In prayer above all we give Him love and choice. The Latin for love is *di-lectio* – '*De*' – 'out of', or 'from amongst.' '*Eligo*' – 'I make choice of' – i.e. Love is really making a deliberate, *willed* choice of God out of all other things. I think that is all the very greatest help and brings real light and great comfort.

It makes one see how a dark, distressful prayer, full perhaps of distractions, can yet be an act of pure love of God when we separate ourselves instantly from the distraction when we realise it and turn at once back to Him.

Yes, this is your time of recollection, of retreat, of steeping your soul in God's Love, of learning to trust Him even unto folly.

Again, Pauline child, you *are* on the right path. Be at peace about that. And I am entirely sure it is all God's drawing, and that Our Lord wants it.

You are not getting carried away by your imagination, but by God's sure drawing of your soul.

Fix a time for your prayer. Say half an hour in the morning. And keep to that. Do not relax it when prayer is cold and dull and suffering. That point is of really great importance. When prayer is easy or when He seems to ask more, you can add to it according to circumstances. And when He gives those impulses of love, do not be afraid to respond: I mean do not fear to let yourself be drawn because you are unworthy or unfaithful or immortified. You are! I am! But Who can most swiftly work that change? Who better knows the depth of our weakness than He Himself Who deigns to draw us to union with Himself.

Carry on with the cigarettes and the good wines etc. These, for you, come in the duties of your state. Just keep the deliberate act of surrender to God in a small denial of yourself [with] one less, according to circumstances.

As regards vanity. Your positive vocation in life is to be a well dressed, well groomed woman. For the love of God (said with a smile & a wink!!) do not be turning yourself into an old 'frump' as an act of penance!!

We all love admiration & attention. For you, it is a positive duty to get it. So just let God use you. Abnegate it to Him in your will at least: tell Him you take it *for Him* & if it were His way with you to take it all from you, that you would still love and praise Him with all your love.

Every time God makes us see more clearly, we see ourselves a little more as we really are, in the light of His Love. And thus we see how little progress we have made.

Never mind that ladder, Pauline. God can lift us beyond the 1st or 2nd rung even from lower than the base, at any moment He wills – provided He finds *di-lectio*....

Loving prayer. Go on just as you propose – without strain and in His Peace, asking Our Lady to hold you wide open for Him....

By this time Georges's rank had already been raised to Canadian Ambassador to France, and this promotion meant that for the first time in several years, a clear future lay ahead for the Vaniers. It meant an eventual return to Paris. In the meantime D-Day came on 6 June. The Allied bombing of towns throughout Normandy and the retreat of the Germans from France began. The news was horrific, however – the scorched-earth techniques of the departing SS troops (who, in one village, locked hundreds of townsfolk in a church and set fire to it) – reached the ears of the inhabitants of Algiers, who heard, as well, of the Allied casualties and the destruction of towns as they fought their way through France.

By July it became clear that the Allies were gaining ground sooner than expected and preparations were made to leave Algiers. Charles de Gaulle left for France in August, and shortly afterward Georges and Pauline flew to London to prepare for their own return to France.

In the meantime, not realizing that advances were being made so fast, Mother Mary of the Cross wrote another long letter to Pauline in Algiers on 22 August:

I rejoice with you that God's loving is drawing you so closely, so surely – and since it is the gift of His Love, we can both rejoice that, when you wrote in June, *Les sentiers etaient encore fleuris* [the paths were still strewn with flowers].

Your will He asks – your loving will in His Hand in all – in shower as in sunshine – so just rejoice with Him 'in the Heaven of your soul' where dwells the ever tranquil Trinity.

He tells us Himself, and what words are like to His own, the words of the WORD of God: 'Abide in Me'. 'If anyone love Me He will keep my word, and my Father will love him and We will come to him, and will make our abode with him.' 'In this is my Father glorified, that you bring forth very much fruit and become my disciples.' And it is in prayer that grace comes to us and is deepened, and by prayer & love & the sacraments do we make our abode with Him within our soul where the Kingdom of Heaven is.

This 'life of God within' is the essence of Carmel teaching.

Go on peacefully then and prayerfully making your soul His sanctuary, His resting place, where He knows He will receive only pleasure. 'God in me and I in Him.'

It is joy to me to think of you in your present most unusual surroundings with God asking from you so very clearly a fragrant love, a loving adoration and a simple praise, in union with Our Lord's own in Mass.'

In an earlier letter Mother Mary of the Cross had rec-ommended to Pauline the spiritual classic *The Cloud of Unknowing*, and she now expounded on her recom-mendation:

> And now the *Cloud*. This is all the same teaching as St John of the Cross – and in fact they are very similar. God, pure spirit, is so infinitely beyond our finite thought that we cannot 'know' Him save by 'not knowing'. And thus one comes to the very same thought as St John of the Cross in the famous Chapter 13 of book I of the Ascent and then in Book II and III – the mind emptied of cre-ated images, the will of affections – this the path by which we come to the knowledge of God, by which we know that we do not know....
>
> The language of the *Cloud* is powerful, nearly poetic – & most captivating. "The meek stirring of love." "Prayer is nought but a devout intent directed unto God." "The little word SIN that stands for all evil – the word GOD for good." "And therefore for God's love govern thyself discreetly both in body & in soul and get thee thine health as much as thou mayest..' 'Look now forwards & let the backwards be."

And in Chapter 43 his whole doctrine set out, beginning 'Look that nought work in thy mind nor in thy will but only God etc.'

I am delighted you love the book as you do & that you have the help. Draw quietly from it all that God means. Sometime later on I will send you a brief setting out of passages with the same ideas in Our Holy Father.

About prayer. Remember always pray as you can & as God draws you to prayer. In silence is our best adoration.

Give yourself a few moments of real silence in which you think of nothing but God – or rather, just turn to Him in love.

No need to remind you that the first fruit of your prayer must be generosity in the duties of your state of life. And those, I fancy, my beloved Child, may very soon be truly exacting.

Let us both strive to say a loving 'Yes' to God – and by joyous love of Him to strive to forget self (self hates that: it 'enjoys' contempt in a sense because that centres on it – but forgetfulness leaves self starved!)

You will have many a humiliating disappointment in your own soul at many a failure, at the vast difference between desires & achievement.

Bear all with gentle patience which is real humility – for impatience is pride, pride that trusts so much in itself & brooks no failure. God, however, for very love of us allows us to fail. We even

compel Him to let us fail, for pride 'stinks' before
Him & in His mercy He will do anything to pre-
serve us from pride ...

On 24 August news came of the liberation of Paris, and
there was jubilation in Algiers. 'PARIS IS LIBERAT-
ED!' Pauline wrote to her children. 'We heard it yesterday noon and I don't mind telling you that all day yesterday we all behaved like lunatics. Last night just by
chance we had five men of the resistance to dinner; two
of them had got away from prison camps in Germany
a year ago and had worked in the resistance afterwards,
until one of them was caught by the Gestapo, was put
into the prison of Fresnes in Paris, but was got out by
his colleagues. I don't think that I need tell you what
sort of evening we had. It was quite delirious. I kissed
them all (shame on you, Mummy), even a Jesuit Father
(more shame, Mummy).'[31]

On 2 September, Georges and Pauline Vanier left
the palatial splendour of their Mediterranean villa for
the last time and boarded a plane to London, en route
to the newly liberated Paris. In London, the Vaniers
met an unexpected restriction: because of the necessity to keep airplanes available for military personnel,
only those in uniform were allowed to travel to Paris.
Georges wore his Canadian army uniform, but Pauline,
clearly a civilian, would have to remain in London. A
solution was soon found courtesy of the director of the
British Red Cross: he gave Pauline the title of convener
of Red Cross activities in Paris, and so, clad in an official

Red Cross uniform, she was allowed to board a plane to Paris. The result of this subterfuge was that before long, Pauline would actually find herself doing what she had hoped to do all along: to be of service for those suffering the effects of war.

Although the towns of Normandy were devastated and green fields were punctuated with bomb craters, Paris, unlike London, was basically unscarred. Pauline, always conscious of fashion and aware that vanity competed with her yearning for deeper prayer, was pleased that she was wearing a uniform. The Vaniers settled into a furnished flat, and their food, American army rations, was simple and monotonous. But it was plentiful, in contrast to that of working class people, who suffered from hunger and malnutrition due to high inflation and the Nazi policy of sending French-grown food to Germany. 'There is going to be a lot of work to do and I am pleased of it as I am longing to get my teeth into something really worthwhile,' Pauline wrote to her sister-in-law. 'We know the people that we don't want to see and the ones that we do want to see, which makes things easy.' She added that they were avoiding 'the smart set - that I promise you!' [32]

Almost immediately she began sending pleas to Canada for food and clothing. Meanwhile, there were tours to see first-hand what more than four years of occupation and war had wrought. On 11 November Mother Mary of the Cross wrote, 'It is indeed wonderful how God has been quietly preparing your soul for your very big work for Him in Paris.' She added, 'Pauline dearest, if you have not yet been to Lisieux go there as soon as you can to put your work in France in the hands of Our Lady Immaculate Queen of Carmel and of our loved St Little Thérèse – Georges and you together. Be sure to write beforehand to Mother Agnes and I will write to her to tell her that you bring our love and prayer to her and to all her dear Carmel.'

It would be several months before the Vaniers were able to make their way to the Lisieux Carmel and have their reunion with St Thérèse's sisters. Pauline and Georges now had their vocation of service cut out for them as an ambassadorial team.

THREE

Thirsting for God: 1945-1952

'When Our Lord lifts us up like that and draws
us, we see ourselves a little more as He sees us
and we have the grace to realise our nothingness,
and what you do is just the right thing: plunge
more deeply in His Love, turning from self,
learning so truly that without Him we can do
nothing.'
Mother Mary of the Cross to Pauline Vanier,
7 September 1948

Post-liberation diplomatic life in Paris was downscale
and prosaic, with 'cocktail receptions' taking the place
of dinners. Hot water was hard to come by, and the fuel
shortage meant that there was little indoor heat during the winter of 1945. As in Algiers, diplomats, generals and prime ministers came and went, and as was
often the case, Pauline found herself frequently lunching and making small talk with leaders such as Winston
Churchill and Field Marshal Bernard Montgomery.

In France, the Allied bombing had forced many
people to live in caves and cellars. Across the country, fuel and food were in short supply, and in some
areas, nearly non-existent. Children in particular suf-

fered from malnourishment, and many were severely anaemic. Desperation was everywhere; nearly everyone the Vaniers knew had family members in concentration camps and had received no word about them.

The role of Canadian Red Cross representative that Pauline had fallen into provided the opportunity for the service she had longed for. She lost no time in learning the country's needs for food, shelter and clothing. At first, her days were divided between writing begging letters to Canada and England and visiting Canadian troops on leave. Soon hundreds of letters descended on her desk with pleas for help.

Attempts were made to answer every letter, either by Pauline herself, or by her secretary, a young resistance member. But the needs were overwhelming, and Pauline castigated herself for impatience and for not being able to provide more help. On 7 March 1945, Mother Mary of the Cross wrote:

> I am so proud of your chances to do God's work in this agitated world. And never mind those faults and failings that you are conscious of. God wants to be loved and served by you, as you are, with all your weak humanness and *not* by an angel! So rejoice that He uses you and lift up your weakness to His Mercy – your misery that gives scope to His Miseri-cor-dare.
>
> Try afresh – for even a very few minutes daily – to 'be still in your soul & see that He is God.'

> You cannot help being distracted in the hectic
> life you are obliged to lead as a duty of your state
> but you will give Him so much pleasure by just
> the loving glance of your will to Him.

V-E Day, 15 May, the day celebrating Allied victory in Europe, was observed in a subdued manner in Paris: French collaboration with the Germans was still too fresh a memory and the country was still too demoralized and impoverished for a spirit of exultation. As well, revelations had begun to emerge about the conditions in the concentration camps in the east. Georges Vanier had discovered for himself the state of the Buchenwald camp in April when he travelled there to find information about three Canadians who had been executed there after being captured on special missions. He sent a report back to Canada with details of the horror he found there and relayed his findings in a broadcast for Canadian radio: 'May I ask you to take my word that these things, however ghastly, are true ... How deaf we were then to the stories of cruelty and the cries of pain which came to our ears, grim forerunners of the mass torture and murder which were to follow.'

He went on to describe in detail what he saw: blackened bodies inside the cremation ovens, noise-making machines that drowned the screams of the torture victims, naked bodies 'piled like so much cord wood.' There were several hundred children, most of them identified as Polish Jews; 'some had been in prison camps for years. Those of ten and over worked as slave labourers on munitions. Not one so far as I know, had any idea of where his parents were; in view of the barbarous treatment inflicted on Poles and Jews by the Germans, it is probable that all are dead.' [33]

As one camp after another became liberated and thousands of French inmates were returned to their homeland, a Paris repatriation centre was installed in a hotel. Pauline went to the centre every afternoon. 'I saw a few that had just got back by plane,' she wrote. 'Most of them were in a frightful physical condition, so thin and weak that they could hardly walk; their shaven heads and their diaphanous faces are pathetic.' [34] And to her mother she wrote that the spectacle of the deportees from the camps continually haunted her. 'This is truly the bursting out of evil in all its horror.' [35]

For Pauline, the demand in the face of so much broken humanity began to tell on her nerves. Mother Mary of the Cross wrote on 28 June:

> Our Lord knows all about the nerves, my Pauline. And indeed no wonder you are strained. But see Him behind every call, & do just what you are doing. Tell Him your love and loving adoration of Him all the time. But on the other hand, you must do something for the nerves. Is a rest not possible?

In the same letter the Carmelite indicated that a rumour about Georges had reached the Hitchen Carmel: that he might become the Governor General of

Canada (this was to happen eventually, in 1959). With characteristic delight, and disregarding probability as well as English law, she wrote, 'My Pauline – honours are coming to the right quarters so delightfully. The only thing further will be for Byngsie to marry Princess Elizabeth & thus you would both be one day the in-laws of England's Queen. Bless you both.'

By the summer of 1945, diplomatic life in Paris was coming back to normal. Travel became easier to manage as well. The Vaniers made their long-anticipated trip to visit the sisters of St Thérèse in the Lisieux Carmel during this time. In addition to her work in Paris, Pauline also accompanied Georges on visits to Canadian soldiers' graves and to towns that had been liberated by Canadian troops. She managed a visit to England and the Hitchin Carmel in late July. There, she spoke of her experiences so far: the victims of the Nazi regime who returned daily to Paris in the form of refugees, prisoners of war and concentration camp survivors. On 6 August Mother Mary of the Cross wrote:

> You were so sweet on Friday, your dearest self, yet a Pauline who had suffered and had faced much stark horror. It came to me so surely while I was listening to your experiences that you must view your life surely from this viewpoint: nothing in it can ever be an obstacle to God in your soul. All is God-ful for you. Parties and all are, for you, *God's* work....

You and Georges seem to me to have a quite
unique 'job' for Our Lord. May His peace be over
you both in the doing of it, more specially in this
unpeaceful world of today.

As stability began to return to Paris, a Canadian embassy was established, and a residence for the ambassador's
family was found. Now began the family's postwar
plans. Nearly eighteen, Jean was coming near the end
of his schooling, and he was scheduled to go to sea with
the Royal Navy. Twenty-two-year-old Thérèse, yet to be
demobilized, had expressed a desire to study medicine.
In Montreal, Bernard, at nineteen, made plans to leave
for France with four-year-old Michel. Twenty-year-old
Byngsie too was waiting to be demobilized, but had not
yet expressed plans for his future.

Much had happened in everyone's life over the past
few years. The four oldest children were now young
adults. For Pauline, still busy with refugee work and
Red Cross responsibilities, there was almost too much
emotion at once over the reunion with her children,
especially with the need to become reacquainted with
young Michel. On 29 October, Mother Mary of the
Cross wrote: 'I know you are having a difficult time
within and without. Despite no 'feelings' and even in
the midst of this inescapable rush in the world, keep
the depth of your soul in His peace. He works in peace.
And I want Him ever to be free in your soul as in a land
all His own.'

At the end of the letter she wrote, 'Will you give yourself from me a book that will help you much, *Difficulties in Mental Prayer* by Boylan. Publishers: Gill, Dublin.' This book, by the Trappist monk Eugene Boylan, had recently been published and was to be the first of several written by him. It was Georges, rather than Pauline, who would eventually discover in *Difficulties in Mental Prayer* the spiritual help he needed. The couple took their 'half hour', as they called their private prayer time, separately. Georges took up his practice of driving to the Blessed Sacrament chapel on rue Cortembert as much as time permitted. Pauline slipped away, usually in the morning, for her private prayer, but the exercise of it, combined with daily Mass, was taxing. On 7 December Mother Mary of the Cross wrote:

> I am so sorry that you are suffering so much. But I do think you ought not to be unduly troubled about the spiritual part. It all seems so entirely clear to me. You are utterly overstrained & for one thing, I am *sure*, you should for the next three months only go to Mass say *twice* in the week. Take this as an order please, my Pauline....
>
> You must indeed, my Pauline, be the sweet mother of your dear & very charming family so do just all you can to relax. Quite simply & peacefully, let *that* be your prayer to Our Beloved Lord and thus you offer Him the best prayer, the duties of your state of life all His...

As you will not be going to Mass, just when you
wake be careful to unite yourself to the Masses
being offered at that time and thank Our Lord for
all His love and mercy. Above all, keep your soul
in His peace.

Pauline's life was now more full of activity than it had
ever been. The emotion in having her family almost
intact, the ongoing Red Cross work, the regularizing of
the diplomatic life, the postwar turbulence of the de
Gaulle government as it tried to establish itself in the
wake of the German occupation and the Vichy regime
– all combined to take an increased toll on Pauline's
nerves. Mother Mary of the Cross wrote on 15 January
1946:

You were tired out and strained. May His Love &
His Peace fill your soul and from that 'cell' of His
love radiate forth on others.

What work He can do through you! I am completely convinced that you and Georges have a
mission for God– quite ahead of your job for Canada!!

Try not to get your life too crowded, as it must
strain you. I know you cannot do much to help it.
But do what you can. It is sheer strain that makes
you porcupine-ish....

I think of you with Our Lady in the Epiphany
Feast. She was indeed the 'Monstrance of Jesus'
then, and so must you be by holiness of life and

sweet gentleness in your own lovely home circle
as in the broader sphere of your life. Make it your
song of praise & love to Him for all He has lav-
ished on you, and I am praying with you both.

Byngsie arrived in Paris early in the new year of 1946,
having been demobilized from the Canadian army. He
and the other two older sons had grown tall, like both
parents. In his studies he had shown an interest in philosophy, and his parents had urged him in letters to
continue his studies in England and France, his father
advising him to apply for a Rhodes scholarship and his
mother writing, 'we have many friends who are quite
adequate in that line, amongst others [Jacques] Maritain and [Etienne] Gilson' [36] At this point, however,
Byngsie was happy to be reacquainted with the family and to help with odd jobs around the embassy and
assist as aide de camp to his father on official occasions.
It was unclear, however, what the young man planned
to study. Shortly after Byngsie's arrival, Pauline wrote
to her mother about how spiritually mature and refined
she found her son: 'He's really a soul chosen by God,
and if God wants him for Himself, it would be disgraceful for us not to give him generously.' [37]

Early in 1946, the Vaniers discovered the historical
town of Vézelay, in Burgundy, south east of Paris, which
they were always to regard as their spiritual home. The
town was built on the side of a hill, the houses and
streets interlocked in labyrinthine complexity. The
main street ended at a twelfth-century basilica, which

stood at the top of the hill. The town had been one of the starting points for the medieval pilgrimage to Santiago de Compostela, as well as the second and third crusades. The basilica had been built in precise synchronization with the solar cycle, so that at the winter solstice the noonday sun would shine on the capitals of the north pillars and at the summer solstice it would stream straight down the centre of the nave. A park behind the basilica, which was lined with beech and oak trees, gave out on a wide vista of the forests, cultivated fields, and villages below. The Vaniers eventually leased a house near the park. This setting provided a sense of peace and beauty for the rest of their years in France, and even afterward.

Late in the evening of 20 August 1946, Byngsie knocked at the door of his parents' room as they were getting ready for bed. There was something he wanted to tell them, he said, before the day was over. The significance of the day was immediately apparent to Pauline: it was the feast day of St Bernard of Clairvaux, a Cistercian luminary. Their son announced that he had decided to return to Canada to enter the Trappist branch of the Cistercians in Oka, near Montreal.

In the first week of September Byngsie and his parents spent a few days in Vézelay, and in personal notes, Georges recorded that he and his son walked together through the park among the enormous trees and sat on the wall overlooking the valley. He asked his son what his friends would think of his decision. 'They will think

I'm a crackpot,' the young man replied. [38] To Pauline, Mother Mary of the Cross wrote on 11 October:

> I am with you in loving prayer so closely these days, when God's Love is asking you and Georges so great a sacrifice even while giving you so great and privileged an honour.
>
> And in all, He gives you the great flood of grace for this holy Present Moment – a grace He destined for you on the day when you received the precious Sacrament of Holy Matrimony.

On a week-end trip to Vézelay in early September, Georges jotted down a record of a talk with his son:

> Yesterday afternoon Byngsie and I went for a walk – it was more a stroll and in its course we sat on the wall which commands a wondrous view over the valley.
>
> I asked him about formalities connected with his entry to the monastery, dowry or payments for accommodation etc. He said there were none, in any event not during the probation period, which lasts one year, at the end of which the simple vows are taken.
>
> I said I was very glad he had entered [sic] Oka Monastery, and was identifying himself with the past of his fathers. Oka was very near Montreal and on the lake at the other side of which, at Seun-

evillle, was the house in which the Archer family had lived for many years.

He replied that it was the normal thing to do, that God's Providence worked through normal channels as a rule. When little St Thérèse entered, she simply went around the corner at Lisieux.

I said that having travelled a little and considering his intellectual attainments he might have been attracted to other places of greater beauty or learning. I repeated I was glad, however, he had entered near home where, with the troublous times ahead, he might find himself later to be in a position to render service not only to God but to his fellow men as well. (This remark was inspired by the feeling that at some future time the religious life of Quebec for clergy as well as laymen may have need of men possessing his peculiar qualifications of race, language, intellect and with God's grace, of holiness.)

He replied that to look for something 'fancy', to choose a place to enter because of Gothic arches, was in itself disturbing. The word he used was not disturbing but the sense of his remark was that if such considerations influenced one's decision, this might cast a doubt on the genuineness of the vocation[39].

In mid-October, the weekend before the young man's departure, Georges, Pauline and Byngsie returned for a final trip together to Vézelay. Georges observed his son during Mass in the chapel of the great basilica as the early morning light illuminated the sanctuary: 'Byngsie in his army jacket and battle dress trousers. He knelt, head slightly bowed, hands in front. At communion I was only a few feet from him and looked at him as he received communion, eyes closed, expression of great serenity,' he wrote later. 'I felt in the chapel that I was saying good-bye.' [40] Georges and Pauline had from their first visit to Vézelay established the custom that, on leaving to return to Paris, they turned to look back as the car descended the hill away from the town. The gesture signified a literal 'au revoir' – 'till the next time' – to their spiritual refuge. On this occasion, they decided they would not look back at Vézelay as they were leaving; the son in the car with them would never be making this trip again.

Byngsie left for Canada on 21 October, a month before his twenty-first birthday. Georges wrote to his son upon his leaving:

> As you leave my heart is full of gratitude to God for His gift to us of you who have given to our union in the Sacrament of Marriage a sense of holy fulfilment. He has now called you: being what you are you answer, 'adsum' ['here I am']. In doing so you have made us very happy, Byngsie, yes, very happy.
>
> We will miss you but we will not lose you. You will be nearer to us than if you were with us in

body. This I believe very deeply. There must be no sadness in the parting.

I shall never forget the last two days at Vézelay. Your kindness, your silence – the comfort you gave us as if we and not you, in the fullness of youth, were making the great sacrifice so repugnant to human nature.

I know it must be infinitely hard to give up all of and in this life – but you have hidden your suffering that we might suffer less. Thank you, dear, for making it easier for us.

God bless you, Byngsie, the best of sons. [41]

Two weeks later,, Georges and Pauline returned to Vézelay for the weekend, apprehensive lest his absence loom too large for them. The weather was cold and damp, and during the night they filled gin bottles with hot water to heat the bed. They retraced the places they had been with him 'but we were not uneasy or sad', Georges wrote in his notes. As the car left Vézelay on Monday morning, heading down into the road toward the valley, they turned to look back, with the feeling that, as Georges recorded in his notes, 'we have not lost him'.

Byngsie wrote to his parents two days after his arrival at the monastery in Oka. 'Thank you particularly for all you said in them,' he wrote, referring to his parents' farewell letters, 'and more especially for the love and the heart from which it comes. It is a great strength to know your happiness and joy in this move, because you don't stop being Mummy and Daddy because of it. No iron bars or bright lights flash when you cross the bar. Your farewell letters will always be an example and encouragement to me, and I do mean it. And your last sentence, Mummy, gives a carte blanche which no common mother could ever give and a responsibility which would well make one quake but for His help. Casting everything else aside (which you have to do, as much for common sense sake as for any other) I am fairly sure that this is God's will for me, and I know it will be a strength for you too to know that from then on, you go from second to second (i.e. almost from bell to bell).' [42]

On Gaudete Sunday, December 15, he wrote to his parents for Christmas and added, 'Another reason why this is Gaudete day is that our Father Abbot gave your little one the habit after the morning Mass. I can't yet know all that it means, and the only thing that keeps me from fading away in fear and trembling is the conviction that it is the will of God, and, if you like, the responsibility is His, and so He can't complain. Pray, though, that Br. Mary Benedict follows suit, without fail and without hesitation, because it is strictly a two-handed affair. That is my new name, which you will be anxious to know, you may have already held a sweepstake on the matter.' [43]

The move into the monastic life would not be an easy transition for the newly-named Benedict. Pauline had concerns about her son's health in the face of the austerities practised among the Trappists. Benedict tried teasingly to set her mind at ease: 'Because,

Mummy, you may be worrying or wondering (Daddy, you have a more Cistercian outlook on monastic life!) – please know my health has never been better; our Father Abbot is a real brother and Father in your place.' [44]

A friend with whom their son had stayed in Montreal during the short time before he entered the monastery wrote to Georges that the young man was 'a uniquely gifted, graced, and translucent soul called to go arrow-straight to God'. He continued:

> I am convinced that he is doing the right thing. Byngsie knows the whole meaning of life, he realizes what is at stake, and he is moving up to his rightful place in the front-line trenches of the Church. His great gifts will not be buried at La Trappe, they will fructify and radiate, bringing strength to the whole world.' He added, 'His decision must have brought you piercing sadness. So much sacrifice and so many divisions have been necessary in your closely-knit family, and now you and Mme Vanier are asked to pay a price greater than all the others. But what deep consolation and joy it will bring you. This is your greatest sacrifice and your greatest accomplishment. What a grace it must be to be the parents of Byngsie. [45]

Three years later a letter from the same friend suggested hints of some of the difficulties that Benedict had encountered in his initial period: 'I don't mind confessing to you now that the last time I saw him over a year ago I was a little worried. There was a slight impediment in his speech, and I sensed a certain tenseness. One was aware of the price he was paying. Now all that is gone. He looks splendid. He radiates peace, sanctity, and health. Although lean, he is clearly adequately nourished. He has, I think, hit his stride. He was of course subdued and restrained in manner – but he was the old Byngsie, full of humour and fun.' He went on: 'I have never met such purity, candour and humility. And we laughed because we were happy, because who could be sad when held in the Everlasting Arms. And as I looked at Byngsie I felt all my own cheapness and superficiality and cynicism falling away. There is nothing but God, no happiness but to do His Will. How clearly this is seen reflected in Byngsie's eyes. For he has chosen the better way.' [46] (In the summer of 1952, however, Benedict would be hospitalized with tuberculosis for two years.)

The young Trappist himself gave an explanation of his silent Trappist vocation to a family friend who had written asking for prayers and advice: 'You can count on the prayers of the community; and you know our vocation is not so much to give advice – so often without full understanding or sympathy – or to make lengthy dissertations, as to offer our lives in silence for all intentions known or unknown which the Good Lord wants to bring about. The light and the grace are in His Hands, not in ours, and so we will try to give our daily lives for His intentions and yours, and He will do what is best. You do know though, that this is not just a formula, but a conviction that the real help, light, encouragement, strength, courage, faith come from Him, and that often we hinder when we think we help.'[47]

Their son's decision to enter the Trappist monastery in Oka, rejecting everything that spelled worldly success, marked another profound spiritual turning point for Georges and Pauline. Each of them, in different ways, would rely upon his help – usually from afar – for the rest of their lives. Pauline wrote to her sister-in-law, Frances, a few months after his departure: 'Strangely enough although I miss him more than I can say I feel him very close to me. I find him in my heart so near, so real when I pray ... After all why shouldn't it be that through prayer we meet in spirit?'[48]

A few years later, Georges wrote to a friend about his son's decision to enter a Trappist monastery: 'Some of our friends have said, and others hinted, that his retreat into silence represented a loss to the world, that he might have done so much more good by living with his fellow men. All this is true and cannot be other than true unless one realizes that the greatest force in the world flows from prayer and personal sacrifice. The chief counsel given repeatedly by our Lord in the Gospels is 'pray'.'[49]

Meanwhile, although their son's leaving for the Trappist monastery marked a major change in the Vaniers' lives, a number of other important developments also

occurred. In October 1946, a few days after bidding
a tearful goodbye to Byngsie on his way back to Canada, Pauline received a letter from a forty-two-year-old
Dominican priest by the name of Thomas Philippe,
who taught theology at Le Saulchoir, a theological college in Soisy-sur-Seine, south-east of Paris, and who had
established a students' centre near there called l'Eau
Vive:

> Madame.
>
> Perhaps you remember the kind welcome you
> gave me last July when I came to speak to you
> about l'Eau-Vive, our little international centre.
> The warm letter you sent me after our meeting
> emboldens me to write to you again. Would it be
> possible for you to receive me for a few moments
> next Saturday? If you could receive me at the
> end of the morning, this would be perfect, but if
> another time suits you better, I could arrange it. I
> would like to discuss with you practical measures
> to bring some Canadian students to our place in
> Saulchoir, either to live there during the scholastic
> year, or to spend some days in rest and relaxation.
> I would like Canadian Catholic students in Paris
> to be able to consider l'Eau Vive as their spiritual
> home where they will find the best that France has
> to offer ... [50]

Several months later, in June 1947, Père Thomas wrote
again, inviting Pauline to Le Saulchoir for the feast of

Corpus Christi. He added: 'I hope that your son will be able to accompany you. You know that it would be an honour for us, and for me especially a great joy for you to visit the Saulchoir convent, the Monastery of the Cross, and l'Eau Vive.' [51] (The son he referred to was Jean, by now nineteen years of age and an officer in the Royal Canadian Navy. Like his mother, he was exploring ways to deepen his spiritual life. His meeting with Père Thomas would have enormous consequences.)

It may have been at this event, or immediately afterward, that Père Thomas informed Pauline that he was giving a series of conferences at the Carmelite monastery in Nogent-sur-Marne, near Paris, and he urged her to attend them. The discovery of this Carmel dovetailed with a quest she felt for a deepening of her spiritual life and a place to go for silence and prayer. The priest then pressed her further, suggesting that he become her spiritual director. She wrote to Mother Mary of the Cross in considerable consternation, and the nun replied on 18 June:

> I cannot tell you how deeply I rejoice and thank God over the Carmel of Nogent-sur-Marne. That will be a real sort of spiritual life for you, and so close at hand …
>
> About Père Thomas Philippe. I smiled when I got to your sentence about his word putting you off. For each fresh word of yours that I read about him put me off more and more – I might even say, stiffened me up. I do mistrust people who offer

themselves to help the souls of others, and also people who issue invitations to hear them preach. And from that angle I feel on my guard about him still. But his Conference sounds completely beautiful, and I am sure the Carmel there would not have him to give a Conference were he not of very great spiritual help. His youth does not seem to me to matter. The fact that he is a Professor of Mystical Theology would to my own mind be a security and safeguard.

As regards your own soul my thought for you would be to hear him once or twice again, if that is convenient to you, but very definitely without letting him know that you are going to be present. Also perhaps you could go to Confession to him, and here again I would say, without letting him know. If he is going to be God's instrument for your soul you very decidedly do not want to get a sort of personal social friendship with him, if you can avoid it.

Finally I would go very slowly before I opened out to him. Frankly I fancy he is going to help you a great deal, but I do think it is very much better to go slowly in so grave a matter. What comes to me through your letter is that he is slightly rush-ing at you. You can hold that [sic] later on, or you may even have to put up with it. But I think this is the feature that is probably having the same hold-ing back effect upon both you and me.

If after these few precautions all proves right, then open wide, wide to him, and God will give you what He has in store for you, and it should be an immense help in your life. But again I say, go slow at present.

The next day, obviously still concerned, Mother Mary of the Cross wrote again:

On reading over your letter again I feel I have been scarcely strong enough about the caution which I think it would be well for you to exercise as regard to Fr Thomas Philippe. Will you at least take no definite step until after you return from Canada.

Here is my own little experience which coincides so much with how you have felt in this other case, that I just put it to you briefly. My mother became an invalid when I was 14, and died when I was 21. We lived in a parish where the priest would visit, and finally arrangements were made with the Jesuits at Roehampton to come to hear her confession, and bring her Holy Communion. This arrangement was working when I came home from school aged about 15, possibly 16. I cannot quite remember. I loved my mother, as you know, very very dearly, and would have done anything to get her the Sacraments as frequently as possible. One holiday I met this priest, and I am afraid young and all as I was, my personal feeling towards him was almost exactly what you

Pauline Vanier with her first child, Thérèse, 1923. Her first pregnancy ended in miscarriage in 1922. (Vanier Family)

Georges Vanier, left, a newly minted officer of Canada's 22nd battalion, leaving for England with fellow officers, April 1915. (Library and Archives Canada, Georges P. Vanier Fonds, Acc. No. 1971–311)

Georges and Pauline Vanier with their three oldest children, Thérèse, Byngsie, and Bernard, 1928. (Vanier Family)

Pauline with two Carmelites,
Sister Monica (left) and
Sister Gabriel, on the
occasion of the Hatfield
Carmel's move to Hitchen,
Herts, 1938. (Ware Carmel)

The four Vanier boys:
Byngsie, Jean, Michel,
and Bernard, 1941.
(Vanier Family)

The Vanier family in 1940. (Vanier Family)

The Vaniers with Free French officials in Algiers, spring 1944.
Seated beside Pauline is General Leclerc, a distant cousin.
(Library and Archives Canada, Georges P. Vanier Fonds,
Acc. No. 1971–311)

The Vaniers with an unidentified cleric, touring Normandy in
the aftermath of D-Day, 1944. (Library and Archives Canada,
Georges P. Vanier Fonds, Acc. No. 1971–311)

Benedict (Byngsie) as a
young monk, December,
1946. (L'Abbaye
Val Notre Dame)

Jean as a young naval officer,
late 1940s. (Vanier Family)

The Vanier family on the occasion of Benedict's ordination to
the priesthood, March, 1952. Missing is Thérèse, who was
writing her medical exams. (Vanier Family)

Georges, Pauline and Jean with Pope John XXIII, 18 March 1959. (Vanier Family)

Georges and Pauline Vanier in front of the basilica in Vezelay, 1959. (Library and Archives Canada, Georges P. Vanier Fonds, Acc. No. 1971–311)

The inauguration of Georges Vanier as the 19th Governor General of Canada, 15 September 1959. (Library and Archives Canada, Georges P. Vanier Fonds, Acc. No. 1971–311)

 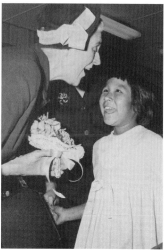

Georges Vanier with Queen
Elizabeth II, Quebec,
1959. (Library and Archives
Canada, Georges P. Vanier
Fonds, Acc. No. 1971–311)

Pauline with an unidentified
child in Yellowknife NWT,
on a tour of Canada's North,
1961. (Library and Archives
Canada, Georges P. Vanier
Fonds, Acc. No. 1971–311)

Georges and Pauline Vanier in the mid-1960s. (Library and
Archives Canada, Georges P. Vanier Fonds, Acc. No. 1971–311)

Georges and Pauline with their grandchildren. From left:
Laurence, Philippe, Valerie and Anne-Marie. (Vanier Family)

Pauline Vanier leaving
Ottawa for Montreal after
her husband's death, April
1967. (Library and Archives
Canada, Georges P. Vanier
Fonds, Acc. No. 1971–311)

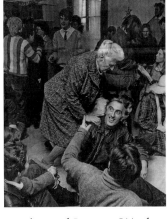

Pauline and Jean at a L'Arche
Christmas party, December
1973. (Jean-Marie Versleege)

Pere Thomas Philippe.
(L'Arche Trosly-Breuil)

Thérèse and Benedict
Vanier in later years,
Oka, Quebec. (Abbaye Val
Notre Dame)

Pauline in an undated
photo. (L'Arche Trosly-Breuil)

Pauline with L'Arche core member, Loïc Profitt a few days
before her 90th birthday. (John Schults)

described in your letter: especially when he prac-
tically asked me to go to Confession to him, and
later on, on two occasions, gave an invitation to my
mother for me to go and hear him preach and give
a conference. We were under a very great many
obligations to him, both as regards my mother and
as regards the interest he was taking in my eldest
brother. But every contact I had with him myself
literally 'put me off', you got the exact right word.

However, I do think the difference between this
experience of mine, and your own feelings about
the French Dominican, was very marked in the
way that the Jesuit in question was not outstand-
ingly holy, whereas you feel Fr. Thomas Philippe is.

This Jesuit suddenly ceased to come to my
mother, and another priest was sent, without
much explanation being given. We wrote to him,
because he had given up a lot of time for my
mother. We got no answers. And then eventually
learnt that he had left the Order. Later he left the
Church. And eventually he married. Finally he set
up a school and was killed in a motor accident. Let
us talk it over quietly when you come to England.

Whatever were the initial difficulties Pauline had with
the zealous Père Thomas, she decided to seek his spiritual advice, and five months later, on 19 November,
Mother Mary of the Cross wrote, more hopefully, 'I
shall be happy for you to have a real spiritual guide
and friend. But just go still a little slowly: then we will

both be sure. I am praying much for this need and intention.' In a later letter she quoted Pauline as saying that Pere Thomas's spiritual direction was 'through prayer and nothing but love', to which she responded, 'you tell me all.' (Many years later the priest-writer Henri Nouwen would describe Père Thomas as 'a man on fire, the fire of God's Spirit. The way he pressed his eyes closed while praying silently, the intensity of the high pitched voice with which he said the prayers, read the Gospel, and proclaimed God's Word, the trembling hands stretched out over the bread and wine, the intimate way in which he gave communion to all who walked up to the altar...were all expressions of a man whose whole being had been transformed by the fire of God's love.' [52])

For the rest of the Vaniers' years in Paris, Pauline continued to regularly visit the Carmel in Nogent-sur-Marne. There she met the prioress, Mère Térèse, who had come from a well-to-do Parisian family and who would become a life-long spiritual support for both Vaniers. On 12 February 1948, Mother Mary of the Cross wrote:

> It is a joy to know that you thirst more & more for Our Lord. And in His closeness to you, you know He is showing you just what you say – that He is leading you on, closer in His Love, in order that little by little He may have more & more love from you, for Himself alone.

Keep His Peace deep in your soul – so that you spread His very life in all your contacts.

Two months later, on 4 April, she added:

The black patch was to be expected. Our Lord so clearly wants your roots deepened in Him. And oh! How I loved to hear of the method of direction mostly through prayer. I rejoice too at the help that comes from the dear Prioress of Nogent. And I just love to know that you find us one, as *should* be the case with two daughters of our holy Mother. And what she told you about reading the work of Our Holy Father, beginning with *The Spiritual Canticle* and *The Living Flame of Love*, is what I myself always suggest.

In spite of the deepening of her prayer life, Pauline continued to feel the pull of vanity and the social whirl, which, given her extroversion, she loved to be part of – and for which she then chastised herself. Mother Mary of the Cross wrote on 25 September:

Even the 'cyclonic turn of *mondanité*' is for you a duty of your state, and therefore, full of God's grace. And when you feel vain, and all the other things that you would wish not to feel, let it just show you afresh your own weakness, and cast you more lovingly into the very depths of His Sacred Loving Heart, where is all Peace.

Six months later she wrote, 'Thank God for His love and goodness to you in so many ways. You have the joy and the grace to have a vocation to special union with Him, within your own holy call to your married state.'

Mother Mary of the Cross had suffered from various ailments since the beginning of the war, and in the late 1940s she was often hospitalized because of heart trouble and bronchial complications, her letters to Pauline written from her hospital bed. In September, 1949, she was ill enough to receive the Last Sacraments and used a wheelchair in order to conserve her energy. In the meantime, Pauline, six years after her director at the Hitchin Carmel had suggested the idea, asked permission to be received as a member of the Third Order. She was received as a tertiary at the Nogent Carmel on 24 November 1949, and was given the Order's brown scapular. She took, rather grandly, the name 'Thérèse de Jésus': the same name as the great Spanish reformer of the Carmelites.

'Carmel is so simple,' Mother Mary of the Cross wrote to her on 20 November. 'It goes so simply and directly to God. Above all in its great devotion to the Incarnation and to the Word made flesh glorifying God by His hidden, suffering and immolated life... May you be plunged deep in Carmel's spirit now and always.'

Pauline wrote that she had come to her reception ceremony with empty hands, to which the English Carmelite responded on 6 February 1950, 'Oh yes! There is indeed a wealth of spiritual teaching in the idea of having our hands empty that He may fill them.'

is indeed a wealth of spiritual teaching in the idea of having our hands empty that He may fill them.'

Jean Vanier's life, in the meantime, was also reaching a turning point. In April 1946, Pauline had written to her mother, 'Jock is in good form and it's clear that the sailor's life was meant for him, or I should say that he's meant to be a sailor!'

The following year, he was chosen as one of the young naval officers to accompany King George VI, Queen Elizabeth and their daughters, Princess Elizabeth and Princess Margaret, aboard the *Vanguard* on their royal tour of South Africa.

This was a high point in the young sailor's career. He sent the family an exuberant account of the trip, describing in detail how he met the royal family: 'I stepped forward and shook hands with His Majesty at the same time bowing my head. He said "How do you do"; and I tried to make some appropriate reply but my voice seemed to stick somewhere down in my stomach, and then moved on [to] the Queen and the two Princesses, they were all smiling sweetly. The whole thing was very awe inspiring, and my legs felt a bit wobbly.'

In Cape Town he danced with Princess Margaret at her sister's twenty-first birthday ball and on another occasion had afternoon tea with her ('it was amusing to see her take tiny little bites out of an even tinier cut sandwich, whilst we were all putting them into our mouths one at a time!'). Later he watched newsreel footage that had been taken on the ship and excitedly reported, 'I was able to see myself on the film!'[53]

Three years later, Jean made the decision to leave the sailor's life behind. In June, 1950, a letter from the chief of the naval staff of the Royal Canadian Navy reached Georges in Paris:

> Dear General Vanier:
>
> You are undoubtedly aware that your son, Lieutenant J.F.A. Vanier, R.C.N., has submitted an application to resign his commission in the Royal Canadian Navy, in order that he may undergo studies in the L'Eau Vive, Soisy-sur-Seine, France, preparatory to entering the priesthood.
>
> With this worthy ambition there can, of course, be no quarrel but I must point out that the resignation of such an extremely efficient and capable young officer as your son is a severe blow to the Royal Canadian Navy, more particularly as we have all too few outstanding French-speaking Canadian officers in the Service.
>
> In view of the fact that your son undoubtedly has a promising career before him in the Navy, I would be most grateful for your remarks or suggestions before I recommend approval of Lieutenant Vanier's resignation to The Honourable, the Minister of National Defence.[54]

Georges replied:

> I have your letter of the 20th June referring to my son Jock's application to resign his commission in the R.C.N. in order to study at l'Eau Vive, Soisy-sur-Seine, France, with a view to entering the priesthood.
>
> I was aware of Jock's intention. I am sensible of your appreciative references to him and humanly speaking I understand and endorse your feelings. Like you I am sad that not more French speaking Canadian officers are commissioned in our service.
>
> But Jock's aspiration transcends the human level. Knowing him as I do, I feel sure that he is answering the Master's call. As you have been kind enough to ask me for my comments, I can only say that this is a matter between God and him in which man if possible should not interfere. I feel it my duty therefore to urge you most earnestly to forward his application to the Minister of National Defence for approval and I would be very grateful to you if you could expedite the procedure so that he may enter l'Eau Vive as soon as possible....[55]

L'Eau Vive had been conceived as a way for postwar students to combine their postwar studies with a spirit of prayer within community. Père Thomas began his explanation of the rationale behind it thus: 'In the midst of a universe divided by war and revolution, beset by all sorts of crises, caught between opposing ideologies, Christians of various countries feel the need to deepen their spiritual life. In doing so, they want to move beyond the barriers that divide them and come together in unity in order to bring to our sick world a spiritual unity that alone can save it.' L'Eau Vive was to be an ecumenical centre of prayer that would accompany the study of theology being taught at the Dominican college of le Saulchoir. 'In the Middle Ages, our fathers built cathedrals of stone,' he went on. 'We want to build, in the heart of France, near Paris, a spiritual cathedral, made of living stones, gathered from the four corners of the world, offering a refuge and a source of living water to all who are thirsty for truth and peace and who want to draw light and the flame of love from it.' [56]

Père Thomas established a fund-raising organization called the Association of the Friends of L'Eau Vive, and for the rest of their time in Paris the Vaniers were at the centre of the organization. At the priest's behest, Pauline tried to interest the other spouses of ambassadors to help in promoting l'Eau Vive, and Pauline's mother contributed to the upkeep of the building. The philosopher Jacques Maritain pledged to spend six months a year teaching there. The Catholic writers Francois Mauriac and Paul Claudel also supported Père Thomas's vision.

Jean moved to l'Eau Vive and began studies in philosophy in September, 1950. Mother Mary of the Cross wrote on 8 September, 'Tell Jock the very uncertainty is giving God glory and telling Him his love, and teaching him that most precious lesson, that the will of God is all.' About herself she wrote, 'He has lately given me the grace to give to Him as He hides behind concrete, from which He comes not forth.'

Mother Mary of the Cross's last letter to Pauline was written on 17 August 1951. She wrote with a shaking hand: 'You know I gave my will and fresh entire surrender to God's will and good pleasure when first I knew I was ill and could not humanly recover … I fail badly in the giving, but that shows His Love and Mercy best.' She died on Maundy Thursday, 10 April, 1952.

At the time of her death the Vaniers were in Canada, having left for Montreal in March to attend Benedict's ordination to the priesthood. The ordination ceremony took place on 25 March in the same basilica where Georges and Pauline had been married nearly thirty years earlier. Pauline wrote to Mother Mary of the Cross from Montreal on 29 March, but the letter was received in Hitchin only after the nun's death:

> How sad I have been to think of your being so ill again and I can only hope that you are not suffering too much. The dear Lord loves you to the extent of putting you on the Cross with Him and you love Him so that you have accepted this offer of His.
>
> You have been with us much during these blessed days. Your cable to Benedict moved him

deeply as it did me. That you should have thought of him when so ill is wonderful. Benedict prayed for you very especially at his first Mass, asking that you may be given the grace of suffering in His Love.

Oh! how wonderful the ordination ceremony was, so simple and so moving. What a privilege and what a grace has been given to us. The first Mass was more than I could have possibly have imagined. The moment of the Consecration was to me the most extraordinary instant of my life. To think that this child of mine had the power to bring our Creator down on the altar there present for us to receive, how mysterious and how wonderful. My impressions have all been so deep that I can't express them, however much I try. But you understand this and I need add nothing.

....The Father Abbot of La Trappe gave Benedict an extra day with us so as to allow him to say his Mass for me; wasn't it thoughtful and paternally kind?

Jock goes back to l'Eau Vive tomorrow and has done wonderful work here during the short time he has been in this country, he is a true apostle and is most certainly inspired. I think that Our Blessed Lord...is pleased with what he is doing.

You know, Mother darling, that I am always so very close to you in the silence of prayer....

Your child in Him and for Him,

Pauline

FOUR

More Deeply in God's Love 1953-1967

'Whoever humbles himself like this child, he is
the greatest in the kingdom of heaven.'

Matthew 18:4

The Vanier couple had hardly returned to Paris from
their son Benedict's ordination to the priesthood in
April 1952 when they learned that l'Eau Vive, upon
which they had been expending much energy, was in
trouble. Without warning, Père Thomas Philippe was
recalled to the Dominican motherhouse in Rome and
forbidden to exercise his priestly ministry. Unknown to
the Vaniers, the Vatican had been viewing the work of
the Dominicans at Le Saulchoir with suspicion because
of the new theological thinking that had given rise to
their research and writing: work that began to consider
Catholic teaching in the context of contemporary life
and the new discoveries in the sciences. Père Thomas
had found himself caught in the maelstrom, and then,
his writing, too, was scrutinized and declared dangerous.
He had viewed Mary as the model of the contemplative
ideal, and his writing was considered too emotional and
highly charged. Tensions also arose within Le Saulchoir

itself and in its attitude toward l'Eau Vive. With Père Thomas's departure, Jean Vanier was now in charge of L'Eau Vive, whose students were no longer allowed to study theology at Le Saulchoir.

Concerned about the position his son was now in, Georges wrote to the Father General of the Cistercians, who made inquiries at the Dominican motherhouse in Rome. There, the Father General was told that the Dominicans wanted no more to do with l'Eau Vive and that 'it is now under the leadership of the son of the Canadian ambassador.' The Father General went on: 'I then asked him if he knew whether there was any-thing with which to reproach l'Eau Vive apart from the personal matters concerning Père Philippe. He replied that he had heard nothing about the manner in which your son has taken on the leadership, but that the whole matter seems to be extremely delicate ... I'm sharing part of this conversation with you because I know that you are worried about the difficult position in which your dear child has found himself.' [57]

During these years, the American poet Robert Lax found a sometime home at L'Eau Vive and became a good friend of the Vaniers. In an undated letter to his friend Thomas Merton (who, as Father Louis, was a Trappist monk at the Gethsemani Abbey in Kentucky), probably written in 1953, Lax wrote, 'I send you a let-ter from Jean Vanier (who is the son of the Canadian ambassador to France & who runs a house for lay con-templatives & students, where I live a lot of the time.) He wonders if you would read a book by his spiritual director Père Thomas Philippe, OP (who was co-founder with Jacques Maritain of this house). The essays are all on the Blessed Virgin Mary & the Contemplative Life, and those I've read I've certainly found good.' [58]

Five months later Lax wrote to Merton again: 'Here too is the letter from Vanier. I have met and talked a couple of times with Père Thomas Philippe and he is wonderful (a living flame) and [a] marvel of sweetness (his qualities are totally communicable).' [59] In a postscript to the letter Lax wrote, 'Can't for the moment find Vanier's letter describing Eau Vive & Père Thomas but will send it soon.' [60] In Lax's subsequent correspondence with Merton there is no further mention of Jean's letter or Père Thomas's book. It is possible that in trying to get a favourable comment from Merton, by now a famous and well respected writer on the spiritual life, Lax was trying to help save l'Eau Vive and have Père Thomas's priestly faculties restored. (Eventually Père Thomas was allowed to minister as a priest again. L'Eau Vive closed, and Jean continued his studies in philosophy at the Institut Catholique, but in discerning his calling, decided it was not to the priesthood.)

In 1953 Georges Vanier was told that he was to be replaced as Canadian Ambassador to France. The postwar period had been intense years of prominent diplomacy on his part, and both he and Pauline were praised highly for their contribution to the rehabilitation of a country that had been devastated by war. He was offered several other ambassadorships, including that of Canadian ambassador to the Vatican, but for various reasons none materialized, and he chose to retire and return to Canada – but not before another traumatic event occurred.

On their way from France through England, Pauline found a lump on one of her breasts, which was discovered to be cancerous. A complete mastectomy was performed, after which Georges wrote to Benedict, 'In my last letter I told you how edifying Mummy had been in her acceptance of a very serious operation and in her abandon to the will of God. She was an example to the doctors and nurses at the Hospital. It was obvious she was carried on the prayers of those who love her, yours not the least, perhaps mainly. In moments like these you are the rock on which we rest.' [61] As for any woman with breast cancer, the experience was devastating for Pauline. But as she often did when beset with serious adversity, she took the surgery in her stride and confidently moved on. (The prostheses had to be replaced over the years as she gained weight, and she laughingly referred to them as 'falsies'.)

Ever since he had discovered the book *Difficulties in Mental Prayer*, Georges had sought out other books by the same author, the Trappist monk Eugene Boylan. Boylan had trained as a mathematician before entering

Mount Saint Joseph Abbey at Rosecrea in Ireland at the age of 27. The monk was said to be both sympathetic to the human condition and frank and down to earth in his insight into a person's spiritual challenges. *Difficulties in Mental Prayer* was published in 1944 and became a success among lay people who were desiring a life of prayer.

For years, Georges had remained resolute but floundering during his time set aside for prayer, casting more glances at his watch than he would have liked. This book by Boylan gave practical guidelines which he clung to. He marked passages that obviously helped to open the door of his own spirit and at the same time provided pathways in prayer using familiar analogies. One such passage in the book: 'In short, mental prayer means talking to God "in one's own words" though one may use no words at all! The paradox arises from the fact that even between human friends who know one another very well, smiles and gestures can speak volumes; they are very much one's "own words".' [62] Boylan followed *Difficulties in Mental Prayer* with a succession of other books, all of which eventually found their way into Georges Vanier's possession, including, improbably (given the title), *The Spiritual Life of the Priest*.

In the early 1950s Georges had begun making jottings of some of his prayer experiences. These were not organized, or in prayer journals, but were dashed down in scribbles with many crossings-out, as if he wanted the record of each experience to be as precise as possible. The accounts are methodical, showing a system that he followed regularly in his periods of prayer: acts of adoration, thanksgiving, love, uttered in stilted and somewhat archaic pious language – the prayer of a man of exacting personality whose training and discipline had been honed through the study of law and through military precision in the extremity of war. And then, as his prayer moves along, he is overtaken by surprise: something within him lets go and the systematic method disappears. What comes upon him are spontaneous utterances, or something concrete in front of him (in one case a cross) that seems to take over his inner being, or a spiritual sensation he can describe only as 'touches of grace' or 'touches of sweetness'. Sometimes there are audible sounds from within him that he describes as 'groans'.

The first of these jottings was written on the feast of the Assumption, August 15, 1952, after a period of prayer that he later indicated marked a pivotal moment in his spiritual life:

> Today, as usual, I started by thanking God for allowing me to come to see Him. Then, as is my custom, I said I had come to adore Him, Creator of Heaven and Earth. After a minute or two (I think but am not sure of the time) I said to Him (a) that I wanted to love Him more and more, (b) that I know He loves me, (c) I asked Him to show me how to love Him as I did not know and needed His help. I then had a surprise; I began to repeat, in a way which was both intense and spontaneous,

that I loved Him – and thanking Him for giving me the grace to love Him thus. For some time I *could not* move on to the next point, but kept repeating that I loved Him and wanted to love Him more.

I even experienced a physical phenomenon which though difficult to describe was very marked, and my heart beat rapidly for a moment. I thought for a moment that – . I never passed on to the next point – firstly I was held back at this moment of love and also had no desire to leave it. The next point usually was that I wished to conform my will to His. After this my custom was to ask for graces for certain persons who were suffering or who need God's help for various reasons.[63]

Why did he not finish the sentence 'I thought for a moment that – '? Did he think that he might be having a heart attack or that some other illness might be upon him? Did he perhaps wonder if the physical movement was a signal for an altered state such as one reads about in the lives of some saints? Did he feel unable to articulate the sensation in words? Whatever his reason, it is clear that something new and unexpected happened during his prayer period of August 15, 1952, that he had a sense of being led more deeply into contemplation.

In a note the following November he wrote about his hesitancy in asking Jesus 'to give me His love with which to love Him, to let me thirst for Him as He thirsts for me, and to hunger for Him as He hungers for me...' He went on:

> This morning however after Communion I lost my hesitation – I felt that Christ was in me and I in Him. He could increase – and I decrease to such a degree that He *could* in time say over me, 'This is my body,' and so it seems to me that I in Him might love Him as He loves me, thirst for Him as He thirsts for me, hunger for Him as He hungers for me – and so with confidence I shall say in future, 'Christ give me Your love with which to love You, let me thirst for You as You thirst for me, hunger for You as You hunger for me.' Thus shall I be able to love Him as He desires – any other way is unworthy of His love for me.[64]

His notes often refer to Christ as his 'beloved', as in this one of 29 January 1953:

> This morning at the rue Cortambert chapel prayer was difficult. In spite of many and fervent appeals to Christ's love, there was no feeling in me, or response from the Beloved. I then turned to Our Blessed Lady and said something like this: 'Please ask Thy Son to grant me the grace to love Him more and more – to remind Him that He said to St Margaret Mary, 'I thirst, I burn with the desire to be loved.' [65] Well, I am here, I am a sinner but I want only to love Him. I want to thirst and

burn with the *desire* to love Him, but not only the desire: I want to burn with love for Him.' This was said only a very few minutes before the end of the half-hour which had been arid. Suddenly I felt a sweet touch which warmed my whole being and stirred me to feelings of deep and loving gratitude to the Beloved and to His Mother.

He sometimes stayed beyond his half hour if his own schedule allowed it. He wrote on 11 March 11 1953 while on an official visit outside Paris:

Yesterday morning at Reims I was in a state of prayer for a longer continuous time than ever before ... I woke up a little after 6 o'clock and at once began loving affective prayer without any effort and continued until 7 o'clock. During the 8 o'clock Mass in the crypt of the cathedral, the same loving affective prayer all the time. After breakfast we returned to the cathedral for our half-hour's 'oraison'. Once again I felt very near, so near Jesus, and this continued during the visit of the cathedral until we got into the car to return to Paris – from 6 o'clock till 11:30 I experienced several touches of sweetness.[66]

On Easter Sunday of 1953 he wrote:

This morning in bed before rising after some affective prayer I found myself asking Jesus to take

me by the hand and lead me through the darkness.
Was it because I read yesterday or the day before, I
can't remember which, para. 1 to 7 of Bk II Chap.
XVI of *The Dark Night of the Soul* or because I am
now ready for the dark night? Whatever the reason, His Will be done. During the day I read the
remaining seven paragraphs of the same chapter
and was struck with St John of the Cross's clear
and convincing explanation of the line: 'In darkness and secure.' [67]

On the feast of Pentecost that same year, while the
Vaniers were on a short holiday in Vézelay, there was
another spiritual milestone:

After breakfast, following 7:30 Mass I meant to
work a little on an address I am to give next Wednesday to the Members of the National Defence
College, Kingston. I went to a room with my
papers and closed the door. Without premedi-
tation on my part, I began to invoke the Holy
Spirit in a way I have never done before, in personal, direct, frank and loving affective prayer. I
am convinced it was the Holy Spirit acting on and
in me. In the past my affective prayer has gen-
erally speaking been addressed to Jesus who has
become a companion. But this morning, invoking
the Holy Spirit, I prayed in an unaccustomed way
also to God the Father and to the Holy Trinity as if
They – as well as Jesus – were Beings with whom

I was establishing a personal relationship. I also prayed fervently to Our Lady. There were many touches of sweetness during this period which lasted about an hour. As it was then 10:15 I went to High Mass in the Basilica, after which I did a half-hour of prayer in church and later about half an hour at home waiting for Pauline ... I have felt a very special call to prayer today, without undue fatigue. My mind goes back to the feast of the Assumption last year, Mary's day of glory, marking a turning point in my spiritual life. So I believe does the Holy Spirit's feast mark one today.

Distractions and boredom were not absent from his prayer times, but even then, there was the occasional surprise, as when he was on holiday in August 1953 at St Lunaire, on the west coast of France: 'This afternoon my half hour in church was arid with many distractions. On coming out and while looking at the tennis courts where there were many players, I experienced sweet touches. How mysterious are the ways of the Lord, at what unexpected times He reveals His Presence.'

On the feast of the Epiphany, 1959, he speaks directly to the Lord: 'Sacred Heart of Jesus, You love me and I love You.' This pious expression remains with him, and he repeats it 'over and over again during the day and at night when I wake up.' Then he adds: 'It gives me much joy': a rare expression of spontaneous affectivity in Georges Vanier's written words.

Unlike Pauline, who had an innate need to speak about her spiritual life with someone experienced in prayer, Georges was reticent about such matters. One possible reason why he kept such meticulous notes about these extraordinary prayer times was that he was hoping to find a priest with a temperament compatible with his own whom he might consult. In 1955 he wrote to Eugene Boylan, hoping to meet him, only to receive a reply from another monk telling him that the priest had been named abbot of another abbey. (In early 1964 Father Boylan died as the result of a car accident, and when he heard of the priest's death, Georges wrote to his abbot in Ireland: 'Although I never had the pleasure of meeting him, I knew him well through his spiritual writings, all of which I have read, in some cases more than once. I feel I owe it to his memory and to myself to put on record this tribute of deep gratitude. It all began curiously enough by my reading in the French version *Difficulties in Mental Prayer* which I picked up at a Carmel in Paris. That was the beginning of an important change in my life.' [68])

———

Settling with Pauline in retirement back in Montreal, Georges was offered directorships with boards of corporations, some of which he accepted. He and Pauline had always been attracted to people on the various margins of society – artists, refugees, prisoners, those living in poor economic conditions and the people who served them, such as the Little Brothers of Jesus – and in Montreal they became involved with the Benedict Labre House, a centre for homeless men that had been founded under the inspiration of Dorothy Day and the Catholic Worker movement.

But nothing gave him the challenge or satisfaction that the diplomacy in a major European country had done, or offered the scope of service he still felt capable of. He became depressed in the face of inactivity and the uncertainty of the future. On February 25, 1959, he wrote:

> Morning – very depressed, suffering greatly. I can't go on any longer, my God, but may your will be done. Asking neither to go on suffering nor to die, but showing nonetheless a preference for complete union with God before much longer, giving voice to the hope that my will be similar to His.

The Vaniers made yearly trips to Europe, where three of their children still lived. On 18 March 1959, on a visit to Rome, Georges and Pauline were ushered into the Vatican and a private audience with Pope John XXIII, who had been elected pontiff five months earlier. It was a meeting of old friends. The Pope, as Cardinal Angelo Roncalli, had arrived in Paris as the papal nuncio to France in late 1944, shortly after the Vaniers' arrival there. They had established an easy friendship based on a mutual love of simplicity and the ability to laugh at absurdities (the five-feet-ten-inch Pauline had often acted as hostess when the short and fat cardinal was entertaining in the nuncio's residence, and the three dissolved in laughter when her husband, arriving solo, presented himself in the receiving line.)

In an interview toward the end of her life, Pauline recalled that shortly after they entered the Pope's private quarters, 'In my indiscreet manner I said, "Jean is outside in the waiting room." The Pope expressed a wish to see him. I got up and said, "I'll go fetch him." The Pope put his hand out and stopped me. He said, "A pope has a secretary." When Jean finally came in, with his great height, the Pope embraced him.' [69]

In a short written recollection of the Vaniers' private audience, the new Pope is quoted as saying, 'I'm sorry not to be able to offer you coffee. It seems as if a pope may not be seen eating, drinking or sleeping. I would so much like to be able to offer you coffee, but if I did, the journalists would know about it, because the walls have ears.' He showed them his private apartment, including his bedroom, which had a window with a series of laths allowing a magnificent view of Rome through which he could look without being seen. When Pauline tried moving the laths aside for a clearer view, he stopped her with a smile, saying that a scandal would erupt if a woman were seen peering out the Pope's bedroom window.

When asked if he found the long morning audiences tiring, the pope replied, 'The Lord has given me a very great grace of peace.'

By the late 1950s the Vaniers had been married nearly forty years. Their life together had become, in its own way, an Act of Oblation to God's merciful love. At the beginning of their marriage, Pauline had wholeheartedly accepted Georges's broken body, and every year on the anniversary of his war wound, she still wrote in various ways of her ongoing love. ('Living by your side is a great grace ... I thank you from the bottom of my heart. Continue to help me in the uphill struggle of the spiritual life. Without you it would be difficult. I love you more than ever.' [70]) He in turn embraced the weakness in Pauline – her anxiety and tendency to depression – while openly admiring her extroverted friendliness. To others they presented themselves as a perfect couple – he quiet, reserved, with a dry sense of humour, she vivacious with a rollicking laugh, both of them keenly interested in the people around them, both of them 'Catholics who lived their religion' as a Canadian diplomat described them. Over the decades, as each embraced the weakness in the other, offering themselves as a married couple to God, they realized more deeply their human frailty and finiteness, and their trust in God grew more profound.

In August 1959 Georges Vanier, aged 71, was named the Governor General of Canada: the representative of the Crown, the first person of French heritage and the first Roman Catholic in that position. The office came with not only honour and prestige, but also arduous responsibilities of long meetings, travel over the great geographical distances of Canada, speeches, and ceremonial duties. He wrote to Benedict: 'Continue to pray that I work for the glory of God, in weakness (I am weak) and in humility (I am not humble). I'm aware that the ordeals and difficulties are numerous, but I trust in the mercy of Jesus and the direction of the Holy Spirit.'

And to Mère Térèse, the Vaniers' French Carmelite friend: 'Knowing that I lack the necessary strength, I can only hope that my very weakness will save me. I say therefore to Jesus, "I place my heart in Yours". He went on, explaining his relationship with God: 'I often have the impression…that He keeps me as it were on a leash. There are times when I feel very strong and sure of myself, especially in public, and this *is* important in front of others. But there are other moments… when I am overwhelmed with a feeling of utter weakness and impotence. In these moments of weakness when Jesus pulls upon the leash as it were, to remind me of my nothingness, I say to Him, "Jesus, I abandon myself to Your merciful Love".' [71]

Another book that had come into his possession was *Abandonment to Divine Providence* by Jean-Pierre de Caussade, a seventeenth-century French Jesuit. The deceptively simple injunction of this cleric to do one's Christian duty and surrender everything to God was a link back to St Thérèse and her little way of trust. From now on, as he left retirement behind and entered a public role, he would confide to those whose prayers he relied on that he was constantly trying to abandon himself to divine providence and trust in God's mercy.

He also began a prayerful reading of St Thérèse's *Story of a Soul*, re-reading it again and again. (By the time of his death he would complete six close readings of *Story of a Soul*, annotating and dating each one.) Echoing the saint of Lisieux, he wrote to Mère Térèse of the Nogent Carmel that he was praying 'to the Blessed Virgin to ask her Son to give me the heart of a child'. [72]

The Vaniers moved into the governor general's residence, known as Rideau Hall, in Canada's capital city, Ottawa, in September, 1959. On 15 September, Georges Vanier gave his inaugural address in the Senate chamber of the House of Parliament. He began: 'My first words are a prayer. May almighty God in His infinite wisdom and mercy bless the sacred mission which has been entrusted to me by Her Majesty the Queen and help me to fulfill it in all humility. In exchange for His strength, I offer Him my weakness.' He ended with an exhortation: 'In our march forward in material happiness let us not neglect the spiritual threads in the weaving of our lives. If Canada is to attain the greatness worthy of it, each of us must say, "I ask only to serve".' [73] It was a proclamation of his intention for his tenure to be marked by an inner quality of the spirit. He chose as his motto *Fiat Voluntas Dei* ('May God's will be done').

The couple impressed their fellow Canadians with their warmth and friendliness. Georges displayed a dry humour that was one of his trademarks, telling man-with-one-leg stories and shaping hoary jokes into anecdotes for speeches and re-telling them at his own expense. On probably more than one occasion, he reminded his listeners that the tradition for the Governor General when he visited a town or a city was to give the local children a school holiday, then he recounted his brand of the story: 'I was particularly touched by the story about a little girl, which reached me in the Rocky Mountains. Following a holiday given in the name of The Queen, she is supposed to have said to her parents, "I like the governor general. I hope he won't die too soon, as I want to save up for his funeral".' On another occasion, after he had received an honorary doctor of laws degree from a university: 'The other day someone must have telephoned Government House to ask if I were really a doctor because I heard one of my secretaries saying "Oh yes, he's a doctor all right, but he's not the sort of doctor that does anybody any good".'

One of their first acts was to turn one of Rideau Hall's bedrooms into a chapel, where a seventeenth-century chest they had bought years earlier became the altar. Mass was celebrated every day in the chapel, and that was where the Vaniers spent their time of prayer. The chapel became the spiritual centre of the house. The house staff remarked in later years on the serene atmosphere, even in times of stress and anxiety. Whenever Georges showed flashes of impatience – a lifelong tendency toward staff who lacked his thoroughness – he quickly apologized.

In these pre-ecumenism days, questions had been raised as to whether Georges, as a Roman Catholic, would be allowed to visit worship spaces of other faiths, and he made his position clear from the outset: 'I shall worship in private life according to the dictates of my conscience, in my particular faith, as is the prerogative of all free men. When duty or circumstances call for my presence as Governor-General at a service of any other faith, you may rest assured that I shall be happy to attend and shall do so with entire freedom.' [74]

Early on in their tenure a decades-old eye problem of Pauline's resurfaced, and as her eyes became cloudy and covered by a thick fog, the staff rallied around her. 'Madame Vanier's trouble with her eyes … was a major factor in much of what went on at Rideau Hall during the early years,' a staff member wrote several years later. 'The trouble was serious and went on for a long time, always getting worse. Her courage in carrying on as if nothing were wrong, and his courage in pretending that nothing was wrong while making sure that everything was done to support her, impressed us all and gave to Rideau Hall a strange yet wonderful fraternity.' [75] (Cataract surgery was performed in 1964.)

For the eight years of his tenure Georges was faced with the necessity for constant vigilance over a succession of minority governments, and the Vaniers together faced a new and unexpected situation that the 1960s brought: terrorist violence and threats in the wake of their native Quebec's push for independence. For the couple themselves, the work involved in their public role was simply an extension of the Christian service to which they had devoted their marriage.

Pauline, however, even as she won admiration for her down-to-earth manner and genuine interest in others, tended toward anxiety about herself and worried about her faults. In a letter of 7 January 1962, her daughter Thérèse, by now a medical doctor in London, addressed her sternly:

> Dear Ma, when you feel yourself lapsing into an inferiority complex, remember a number of things ... What Daddy is today and what your children are today is, in larger measure than you apparently realise, your doing ... It happens to be a fact that (on the plane of the world) Daddy could not have done and is doing without you – even you may concede this. Whether or not Daddy (on the spiritual plane) could be what he is today without your having been by his side for 40 years, only God knows – and I would not be the one to risk an opinion but only mention the force of example and again say that you cannot live with someone that long without marking them very deeply and irrevocably.
>
> You also have a couple of sons who are saints or certainly on the road thereto. You may say that is God's work and theirs and of course it is, but you may remember a certain prayer that you said when ... Byngsie was desperately ill – do you suppose that has nothing to do with it? Do you consider that it is coincidence that Jock met Père Thomas through you? It is all very well, but God's Grace needs its agents ... and you happen to be one of them ... I spare you any more in case

you get a swollen head except to say that your immediate family is only a small part of those who are better in so many ways for coming into contact with you. Now, do you think you could have done what you have done without God's Grace? Hardly. Do you think you could have done these things and go on doing them without the particular human soil upon which His Grace has fallen? That soil happens to be your human gifts, talents, qualities, faults, character and everything that goes to make a human being a particular person and not someone else.[76]

Two years later, they heard from their daughter that their son Jean and Père Thomas Philippe, were 'very busy over some new project which he may have mentioned to you – he only briefly said something to me about it – a plan to set up some sort of house or houses near Compiègne for *des débiles mentaux* – it sounds just like him and Père Thomas. And I hope it works out alright.'[77]

Two months later, as if to allay her parents' concern that their son might have taken on too much, she wrote with increased enthusiasm about Jean's new project: 'I think it is a splendid idea in every way and he is going about it very realistically. I entirely approve, for what that is worth! He's put me on the "conseil d'administration" to make sure of at least one vote! The property he hopes to get (almost settled) seems ideal and the house promising. He seems to have a solid team behind him. I think this sort of thing will do a tremendous amount of good. A philosopher who puts his philosophy into practical practice is so rare, and clearly his colleagues and erstwhile masters consider he is crazy or "irresponsible" and wasting his talents! Clearly also, in time, they will see how right he is and how much more teaching can be done (and thinking too!) by a way of life than by pedagogy or whatever the word is. I know his influence with the young will grow in consequence.[78]

The modest house that Jean opened would soon become known as 'L'Arche'. A newspaper article at the time described Jean thus: 'Tall, thin and round-shouldered, he has the long face and prominent nose of the Vaniers. His clothes are baggy and worn. Heavy lines circle his mouth and eyes, the result of frequent wide grins and a habit of frowning deeply while he seeks ideas or the words to frame them.' The various activities of his life up to that point, the 36-year-old Jean said, had been 'a search for purpose.'[79]

Of their other children, Thérèse had become a medical doctor in London, specializing in haematology (and would eventually bring L'Arche to England). Benedict remained their spiritual mainstay and although his monastery was only a two-hour drive from Ottawa, they were able to see him only infrequently. Michel, who lived in Montreal, and Bernard, in France, had both married, each with two children. Bernard no longer practised the Catholic faith, and this fact, which Pauline accepted serenely, was an ongoing source of parental anguish for Georges, who wrote to Benedict about his worry: 'He [Bernard] has beautiful human qualities – goodness, honesty, sincerity, respect for others and their opinions, but alas, these aren't enriched by the will. It is as if a spring had broken. It's infinitely sad to see beautiful talents wasted – for the moment, anyway. As for faith, I am sure that in God's time, he will recover it. There are too many beautiful souls praying for him for the outcome to be otherwise.'[80]

By the mid-sixties Georges's energy began to wane. He wrote to Mère Térèse: 'As for the future, I'm abandoning myself to divine providence. I'm saying to Jesus, "If you want me to continue serving you, lend me your Heart. Mine alone can do nothing. You can substitute yours if you want. It's an exchange that you have consented to before." … Pray, dear Sister, that I'll be honest with myself when I pray thus. It's so easy to express beautiful sentiments, hoping that the will of Jesus is going to be the same as ours.'[81]

He underwent prostate surgery in early November 1966. Pauline wrote to Mère Térèse: 'Since Georges has been hospitalized I must admit to being completely overwhelmed because in addition to my worry about him, I've had to do the work of two, trying to replace him and see to his voluminous correspondence. But now things are fixing themselves and I'm no longer tired because I'm no longer worried.'[82] She laid cornerstones, welcomed visiting heads of state and gave speeches as her husband convalesced, but did so with a forced smile, she admitted a few weeks later to Mére Térèse, because as the weeks went on his energy did not return.

His heart finally gave out several months later, and Georges Vanier died in Rideau Hall on Laetare Sunday 5 March. His body lay in state in Canada's Parliament Building, and he was given a state funeral. Tributes came in by the hundreds. Acquaintances and former colleagues from earlier years recalled that whenever Georges Vanier was in their presence, courtesy and graciousness always pervaded the conversation and a witty remark, told with a straight face, was never far away. A Jesuit priest who did not know him personally said that Georges Vanier's words and presence reminded him of the Gospel injunction, 'Unless you become like little children....'

Pauline's public grief was followed by the need to make an immediate decision: Rideau Hall, filled with staff and servants, that she had called home for eight years, had now to be vacated so that the new governor general could move in. She decided to return to her native city of Montreal, and she bought a townhouse there. Her husband's manservant at Rideau Hall, Sergeant Yves Chevrier, agreed to join her.

The adjustment was difficult. Pauline's extroversion had responded readily to the hum and activity of Rideau Hall, and in spite of her desire for Christian simplicity, she had enjoyed the attention and pomp of her former public role. No longer did people dance attendance on her. No longer was she surrounded by protocol or official functions that had provided the stimulating opportunity to meet people from various walks of life and visitors from other countries.

Most of all, there was no longer the deep and supportive presence of her husband. The day after Easter she wrote to Mère Térèse: 'From the bottom of my heart I had a sense of 'Alleluia', but tears were flowing the whole time ... Everything is hard, it's Calvary.' [83] Still, as she had done on other traumatic occasions, she displayed an unusual courage and resilience in moving on alone into private life. Two weeks later she wrote: 'The Lord is overwhelming me with graces. I'm surrounded with affection. Now I have to find the path that the Lord wants me to follow.' [84]

For a short time she thought that the path she was looking for might lead to a vowed life within the Montreal Carmel. She found a refuge there often during the next few years, and with the gentle guidance of the Mother Prioress, agreed, in classic Christian terms, that her vocation was to be in the world, if not of the world. In 1967 she would not have predicted where the path would lead her.

FIVE

The School of L'Arche 1968-1972

'This side of the veil will always be more or less
cloud, sometimes more, sometimes less, but
"beyond the veil" is His glory. He lets our heart
touch it a little, be warmed.'
– Benedict Vanier to his mother, March 1985

One of the first things Pauline did upon moving into
the Montreal townhouse that she now called home was
to establish a chapel, as she and her husband had done
at Rideau Hall. Although now in private life again, she
still lived a life 'in society', and was a sought-after guest
and public speaker. She had also established friend-
ships with people to whom she gave spiritual guidance.

Then, alone on her own, at loose ends and still in
grief, feeling her own neediness, she badgered herself
with guilt and an overblown sense of remorse as she
built up an image of her husband's saintliness over
against her own faults. Her Trappist son Benedict,
echoing his sister's letter of a few years earlier, wrote
from his monastery, 'Daddy would never have been
who he was without you. You made an astonishing little "team", family-wise and career-wise. All the responsibility and affection into which he grew – as father of a

family, as husband - would never have been, outside of your presence, life and heart. To say nothing of how he was gently prepared for grace and better understanding of who God is by that same presence, life and heart – yours. So – be at peace. You feel your poverty, your failings, and you are aware – even more – of who he was. But – remember how he was aware of *his* poverty, *his* failings. You more than any other can vouch for that.' [85]

Eight months after Georges Vanier's death, Benedict wrote again:

> Don't be too disappointed in yourself and this period of weariness; you have already caused all to bless God for your standing firm during these months – and that represents much more than we think. Don't be too disappointed – but Mummy, I would suggest (if you will forgive the uncomeliness of the expression!) that you take 'the bull by the horns' and force yourself to react. It is almost a sure way of overcoming at least a part of the lethargy of soul that seizes one.
>
> For instance – plan two or three afternoons a week when, for a set time, you can be busy and helpful (in any manner – it does not need technical capacities!) at a centre of some sort – hospital, home, etc. – where God's good charity is at work; where you can meet others – often quite the poor and lonely – and feel that communion with others as well as exercising it. It is important,

Mummy, that you be able to have such a communion, because it is a communion with Him. It may cost you a little effort to get underway, but it is in such things that His Hand and Heart come to our help. The effort to break the ice is worth the warmth you will at least in part, be able to find, and to give ... [86]

Pauline gradually renewed acquaintance with old friends and followed her son's advice by once again helping out at the Benedict Labre House as well as visiting hospitals and taking up the practice of spending time with prisoners. One year, on her birthday, when a friend asked her what she would like as a gift, she asked for a ride to the Foyer de Charité, a children's home, where she greeted the children and spent most of the time stroking the head of a deaf and blind infant who lay in a crib with his hands bound so that he could not injure himself.

She received several offers of honorary doctorates and many requests to lend her name and voice to various causes. To the request for a speaking engagement, she sometimes accepted, but always with the caveat that she was not well educated and was not confident of her speaking ability. This advance warning did not necessarily stop her from delivering eloquent speeches, however. In an address to the convocation of the Royal College of Physicians and Surgeons of Canada in January, 1970, she began, 'I need hardly tell you how honoured I am today on receiving a fellowship from this college of erudition. My qualifications are nil. In fact, I have made a self-diagnosis and found that I am suffering from a 'shrinking brain and an enlarged heart.'

She went on to exhort her listeners 'not to forget the spirit which is within the body of your patients; the sick need your compassion as well as your science....'[87]

She joined a program for needy children and enlisted the help of the hockey star Jean Beliveau, from Canada's National Hockey League, in providing hockey sticks and pucks for them. She had been named the chancellor of the University of Ottawa and took this role seriously. Several years earlier, she and her husband had formed, as a lasting legacy, the Vanier Institute of the Family, and she remained on its Board of Directors.

During these years, her daughter Thérèse kept her up to date with what was happening in 'the house' that Jean and Père Thomas had established in Trosly. It was clear that Jean's work was blossoming, and soon 'the house' became 'houses'. In 1969, Pauline travelled to Richmond Hill, Ontario, to assist at the opening of Daybreak, the first L'Arche house outside of France. L'Arche was now an international movement.

That same year, her mother, Thérèse de Salaberry Archer, died at the age of 95 in Paris, where she had lived ever since the end of the Second World War. Jean, as the grandchild closest to Paris, had taken on the role of caregiver to his grandmother. Even as she began to sink into senility, she remained interested in Jean's new project, and she gave him money to buy her a house so that she could live in the community as well. It was an untenable proposition, and her grandson was perhaps relieved when Madame Archer died as the house was being prepared for her. The house, left in her will to Pauline, now stood empty.

During a visit to Jean's community at Trosly in the summer of 1971, someone suggested to Pauline that she might want to come and live there with the growing community. The idea had no appeal for her. She was proud of the life Jean had chosen, but she shrank from mentally handicapped people, feeling incapable of communicating with them. She worried that she lived too pampered an existence to be able to take on a way of life that was bound to be harsh and difficult. Still, as she was to say later, 'a seed was sown'.

Benedict's response to the idea was encouraging: 'I think it is wonderful you should seriously be considering L'Arche,' he wrote on 10 October 1971. 'It is a question which (whatever be your final decision) really merits it. After all, we have only one life, and it is the Lord's. A passing to a new phase, closer in many ways to the Gospel message, is a precious opening. We are all going to grow older; that that period be closer, and not further, to the Gospel joy and *dépouillement* [stripping], is a wonderful possibility.' He went on: 'For most people, such an eventuality is about unthinkable; and again, for so many it would meet from the start with no sympathy if it were possible. For you, it *is* possible, and it meets with serious consideration and sympathy.... God's good grace, time, reflection, prayer, will see you through.'

He added the wise caution to his 73-year-old mother: 'Should your decision be positive, the younger you are when you arrive there, the better. In this wise, that *l'adaptation* is measured a little by our youth. And *then* you can follow a beaten track! Always beat tracks when you are young!' [88]

Soon afterward, while Pauline was at one of her regular retreats at the Montreal Carmel, the possibility of moving to L'Arche was on her mind. The gospel reading of the day's Mass was the story of the rich young man who comes to Jesus and asks his advice. Jesus replies, 'Go, sell what you have and come follow me.' For Pauline, it seemed like a personal invitation to move deeper into the life of simplicity and spiritual communion with the poor – a desire that in fact had dogged her all her life. She held an auction of some of her possessions, and offered furniture and family mementoes to her children. The seventeenth-century mahogany chest that had formed the altar in the Rideau Hall chapel was offered to the Trappists at Oka and soon became the altar in their renovated church. She decided to move to the L'Arche community in Trosly for a trial period of six months.

She left for France on 29 February 1972, a month before her seventy-fourth birthday. Trosly, northeast of Paris, was a short drive from Compiègne, the historic town where St Joan of Arc had been captured in the fifteenth century and where the sixteen Carmelite martyrs were arrested during the Reign of Terror at the end of the eighteenth. It was a village of stone buildings, many of which, modest to the point of poverty, still did not have indoor plumbing. In the eight years since Jean had bought his first house in Trosly, L'Arche had expanded beyond Europe and North America with the opening of Asha Niketan ('Home of Hope') in Bangalore, India. In Trosly itself, the community had grown from one house to a community of more than 200 in several homes that they called 'foyers'. The 'boys', as the mentally handicapped men were then called, had come to be considered the core members of the community – in essence, its heart and spirit – and to help them as 'assistants', Jean had recruited young people from North America and France.

The two-storey house that Pauline Vanier had inherited from her mother, across the street from the original house that Jean had bought, was called 'Les Marronniers'. It stood behind large chestnut trees at the end of a long stone path. Inside on the ground floor, a kitchen and dining area led to a back bed-sitting room, to which a bathroom had been added. French windows gave out to trees and a garden where roses, delphiniums and lupins would soon bloom.

The late winter weather was rainy, the skies a relentless grey, the house damp. Soon after Pauline's arrival, she wrote to her cousin Lita Dawes in Montreal, who had recently undergone an operation for cancer:

> It seems such ages since I have left Montreal a fortnight tomorrow, and I feel as if it were a lifetime. It is a difficult adaptation, but is coming and

I have much peace in my heart. Physically I am very well. I walk a lot, do a lot of house work, my house is kept warm. But the weather on the whole has been dreadful, cold, windy and rainy but today the sun is shining brightly and it really looks like spring. I am kept very busy mostly with the assistants who are undoubtedly in need of a granny. There is much suffering among them. It is a hard time for all, but mostly for the Canadians who come from an easy functional life. The hours are long, they seldom get away from the boys and that is very demanding and exhausting. Fortunately there is much praying and praying together, which is very beautiful. There are lots of meetings for dialoguing.

I have still no help, not even a char, but Elizabeth and John Dare[89] are angels of goodness to me and cook, bottlewash and clean, etc, etc. I am hoping to have one of the emotionally disturbed to help; she is a very nice child and very capable, so it may work, although she will be with me only about 5 hours daily.

One learns quickly here the simple way of life. I brought over many wrong things to wear and for the house. I have to buy a lot and everything moves so slowly. When you want a shelf put up or something painted, you wait a month to have it done; the phone has been ordered for me 3 months ago and there is little hope of getting it for some months yet. In a way all this is good for our over efficient and agitated American way of life.

There are gay events such as *la mi-carème* (mid-Lent) when everybody was disguised, some very funny indeed – all were the boys and the assistants; even I was dressed in Jock's oldest clothes, a sort of battle dress with a hood; the boys really thought I was Jock and he (Jock) had a false nose, a mustache, a bowler hat and played the clown admirably. Such hilarity.

There are tragic things happening amongst the patients – depressions, much feeling of rejection....

You know, Lita dear, that I am so close to you, realizing a little, I think, what you have gone through and maybe are – the fears, the pains, the anguish even, when one doesn't know what is happening or what is going to happen. I am praying that by now you are reassured and back home. I am sad to be so far away from you at this time when you need to be *entourée*. But Jesus is close to you, giving you strength, peace, trust. Oh, how I wish I could be able to be near you, to help. But maybe I wouldn't be the one to help. The dear Lord knows best. I keep you fast in my prayer, in my love.

As Pauline had indicated, the first people to cross her path at L'Arche were the assistants, idealistic young people who had encountered Jean and had been inspired by his eloquence and prayerful presence. The social revolution of the 1960s still prevailed, and there was a search for authenticity and new spiritual structures. For the Canadian youth who turned up in Trosly, the Vanier name not only was well known, but had become synonymous with a profound spirit of prayer combined with social action. Not surprisingly, many of the young people who arrived were confused in their efforts to find their way in the unsettled times. At L'Arche, a community still in its infancy and growing at a rapid rate, there was little help in the way of training or acclimatization. The assistants, often having few skills beyond generosity and goodwill, found themselves living in conditions that seemed primitive. Inevitably, they found their way to Pauline Vanier's door.

In writing regular letters of encouragement to her ill cousin in Montreal, Pauline left a detailed record of her first months in L'Arche. A week after her first letter, she wrote again:

> I miss you terribly, as I miss many things. But I do think that Jesus did want me here. It is a suffering place. Nobody seems to escape suffering. Jock says that it is a place of purification, and I well believe it. Even the young who are working here don't seem to escape. In fact, they are amongst the most suffering. I have had a chance to know this as many of them have already come to see me and have poured their heart out; this seems to be my job – a recipient of other people's suffering. I

am trying very hard to listen well and to give some joy.

I have just recovered from a very bad go of flu which completely knocked me out for several days, leaving me very limp; I had a very high temperature and ached all over. But all is well that ends well; it was a chance of a rest, which I think I needed rather badly as I hadn't let up since my arrival, and the activities here are numerous. I'm sure that I overdid it at first, especially after going through a fair amount of emotion before leaving Canada and being rather active there as well.

Last Wednesday I went to Paris for the first time and it was a very trying experience; it was the launching of Georges's biography[90] in French; there were about 200 people and all friends of bygone days, most of whom I hadn't seen for more than ten years. It was a very emotional experience, a little too much so. Fortunately Jock came with me, because I don't think that I could have managed to get through it alone. This will be my last visit to Paris for a long time; it is no longer my life.

I can't tell you how kind the 'boys' have been; I have had several delegations of them bringing me flowers, cakes, etc.; yesterday even Raphaël[91] came and sat by my bed and put his arms around me and gave me a smacking kiss. That is something from him, I assure you. I have been surrounded with love and kindness ... Thérèse has been here and gone. She came over for a meeting of the Federation d l'Arche (India, Canada and the various houses in different parts of France). I didn't see much of her as they were in meetings all the time; however, she was with me for some meals, which she ate on the edge of my bed.

I've been interrupted so many times since I started this that I hardly know where to start again – at least six people have been in to see me, all so nice but it is rather disturbing …

Over the next few weeks Pauline would see more of her daughter Thérèse than she had for many years. Thérèse had been interested in L'Arche's development from its beginning and Jean had drawn her in by inviting her to become a member of the L'Arche Federation. As her interest in the community intensified, she would soon be faced with life-changing decisions. For now, it was a consolation for Pauline to have the company of her oldest child for brief moments from time to time.

Spring arrived toward the end of March, and the appearance of flowers in window boxes softened the grey drabness of Trosly's stone houses. Pauline had by now acquired the services of a general house-keeper, who came in to help her for four hours a day. On March 25 she wrote to her cousin:

….Here we seem to be nearly in summer; the days are really quite warm and the nights cool, absolutely perfect. The flowers are sprouting everywhere. The gardens (not mine) are all looking so beautiful – primroses, primulas, tulips, daffodils, and the wild flowers in the woods are lovely. My garden is having a hard time to get started; the boys are doing it and it is slow-going, like everything they do, poor pets ...

I haven't yet had the honour of having Jock for a meal. Except 2 breakfasts. He certainly is a busy man, and has some pretty difficult problems. I now see what they can be and have witnessed some pretty complicated situations. There are many people of prayer here and the little poor chapel sees many there in deep silent prayer; it is so impressive and very inspiring.

A new young man from Quebec has just arrived; such a good, prayerful boy. I had met him at one of Jock's retreats. Last night he came back from a day in Paris, bringing me a lovely bunch of small red roses and daisies. This is the sort of gesture which is so touching. Life is harsh at times and a bit depressing, but one quickly gets out of that depression by a kind and friendly gesture. The boys are undoubtedly difficult to handle, but also very loveable ...

Bernard and his family were here a few nights ago and they are being so kind and thoughtful to me. I do love them dearly. Thérèse was here 3 days but I hardly saw her; she was so busy with meetings....'

Pauline's 74th birthday, 28 March, occurred during Holy Week, and she continued to be impressed with the wide-ranging exotic experiences of the visitors as well as the sincere devotion of some of the young people. Three days later she wrote to her cousin:

> We're having a very beautiful Holy Week, very different to the one I spent last year at Carmel but with a very special beauty. Last night, Maundy Thursday, there was adoration all evening until midnight, each foyer of boys going in one after the other with their special prayers and special hymns. It was moving beyond words. In the afternoon there was a Mass at which there must have been over 200 people, boys and assistants. Today, Good Friday, there was the same number of boys and assistants, all going to Holy Communion.
>
> We also have had what is known as 'partages', which means a small reunion of about 20, all sitting on the floor (even I am getting an expert at it). A fine Jesuit from Toronto spoke to us about Jesus and passion and suffering in the world; it was quite lovely; amongst the young there was an English girl dressed as an Indian who has lived in an ashram in India for three years; she is so prayerful and lovely; we walked home together a few minutes ago, holding hands and not saying a word; no need of verbal communication. Also, a young Canadian lad who has lived in Morocco....
>
> On my birthday delegation after delegation of boys came to my house bringing me little bunches of flowers. It was so touching. I am now known as

la Grand-mère de l'Arche to all here. The assistants come a lot to see me, and they are all so kind
and trusting with me....'

As the weeks went on, Pauline was establishing a routine that had at its centre her spiritual activity: private
reading of Matins and Lauds from the Divine Office in
the morning, adoration in the chapel in the afternoon,
and Mass in the early evening. Filling in the rest of
the day was the parade of visitors that walked through
her unlocked door as well as the trips to the local general store for provisions. Unknown to Pauline, meeting
the villagers likely helped to ease the tensions that had
arisen between L'Arche and the local inhabitants, some
of whom resented the increasing presence of intellectu-
ally disabled people as well as the growing number of
houses the community was buying in the village.

After Easter she wrote to her cousin:

You know, darling, that you are continually in
my thoughts and in my prayer. Every day I go to
adoration from 3:30 to 4:30 in the little Chapel
Emmanuel and always you are with me there. We
have Mass usually at 6 pm, and you are with me as
well. How I wish I could drop in to see you, but I
DO, I am with you.

If only I could convey to you a little of the
atmosphere which prevails here. It is undoubtedly a very special place filled with the Holy Spirit.
Many strange and beautiful things happen, con-

versations especially amongst the young. There is a lot of suffering, but there is also much joy. So many extraordinary people come and go. Many stay as well. The other day a group of students from Birmingham University came for the night on their way to Taizé and are coming back at the end of this week to stay a little longer so as to get the feel of this place. Yesterday there were some young Belgians who stopped over – and so on and so on it goes. There are many, many Canadians arriving and of really fine quality. Their first contact when they arrive is usually very hard for them. I try to help in this, but it isn't easy for them. Life is harsh in this village. But I find the people of the village much more welcoming this year than in former years ...

Alas the weather has been dreadful; I think we had our summer at the beginning of March when we had lovely sunshine, but since then it has poured and blown cold winds. But my house is well heated. Lots of restoration going on, painting, papering, the garden being really made to look quite lovely – so on the whole I am beginning to feel at home. BUT I am going back to Montreal in the early autumn ...'

In spite of the unfamiliarity of life in Trosly and the various inefficiencies, Pauline had settled in relatively well in her first few weeks at L'Arche. Surprisingly, she did not miss the exciting bustle of big-city life that she had been used to virtually all her life. The constant comings and goings were stimulating for her, as was the infusion of youthful zeal in the community, and it delighted her to see so many of the young people at prayer. She was in awe at the breadth of their education and experience.

But less than two months after her arrival, her frustration began to show, even as she found elements of grace in her life. On 15 April she wrote:

> You know that I am close to you always. My prayer is daily with you and that means my heart is so filled with real love for you. I miss you in more ways than one – our phone conversations always started the days in the right spirit. Here I have nobody to really start my day in laughter as you did always.
>
> Today I really feel rather grumpy. The house is filled with people painting the front room; they are our 'boys'. They have a radio going all the time. Somebody else is painting the window frames so they have to remain open, and I'm freezing inside – the house, I mean! I went to the chapel to try and get some silence and peace and there too, they were hammering, sawing wood, dropping heavy things on the floor above. So, as you see, this is not one of our good days. We have our good and bad ones here like everywhere else. The weather is cold and damp, but there are flowers in the gardens …

Jock and 29 others of L'Arche are leaving Monday for a pilgrimage to Poland; please pray for them as I do think it is a bit of a risk as they travel through East Germany and Czechoslovakia and of course by car and with 12 mentally deficient. I am sure that you are also praying for me. I am in great need of support. I feel so desperately poor and inadequate here.

This is terribly badly typed; it is being done by fits and starts as I am continually being interrupted. The boys drop in just to say hello and so do some of the assistants. It is nice but it is sometimes disturbing if one is trying to get on with something.

How I long to be near you, so that I could drop in on you. We could have some good talks. I would do all the talking (that would be a change, wouldn't it!). But my darling, you know that my flippancy is not really meant. My heart is with you daily, and I give you such a hug and a kiss.

Pauline had also been writing to her son Benedict, but he did not need her frustrations spelled out. In his Quebec monastery, Benedict sensed that his mother was spending her first few weeks at L'Arche going to every meeting, welcoming every person who came to her door, exhausting herself, and as a result leaning toward depression, all with a feeling of uselessness, not knowing exactly what she was supposed to be doing: she was neither a leader, nor an assistant, nor an expert in anything whatsoever. He wrote words of advice on the nature of living in community: 'Community is not made by "sameness", nor by "alwaysness", nor by "uniformity",' he wrote:

> Community is a very mysterious entity – especially when it is community-in-the-Lord and for-the-Lord. It is a work of the Spirit, and the Spirit is freedom, the Spirit is diversity in operation, the Spirit is just like the indescribably delicate movement of the wind. It is also embodied in a certain structure, more or less stable, more or less fixed, more or less open to the immense variety in us and in our work. It is a thing of the heart and soul, of *persons* … If there is an element that is *constant*, it throws that much more vividly into relief what is so magnificently rich and varied in us all … In all event, you have to remain *you*. If you cease being you by trying to be everybody, or if you cease being you by trying to *do* like everybody, then community ceases.'

He went on with a concrete image that had direct application to the L'Arche experience: 'Take an extreme (and wonderful) example: in a community there is somebody almost totally paralyzed. Doing nothing "like the others", living nothing "with the others", nothing in sameness, nothing in alwaysness, nothing in uniformity. That person could very well be the most important factor in the community – the kingpin, the centre. In all event – absolutely *there*, absolutely *with*, absolutely *part of*. And everyone else *there, with*, and *part of*, a little bit by reason of that sick person. It is a question of spirit; a question of finding one's place; not in uniformity but in the diversity of our persons, not in "sameness," but *above* it and *beyond* it.'

He concluded his letter with further wise advice: 'Don't try to do, outside, exactly like the others. There are many reasons, one being the lucid one of health, life and adaptation. Get yourself help, discreet and congenial. And don't forget – your place did not exist before, because you weren't there! Find it, simply, slowly, surely: *sans trouble* ... Take your time, you have eternity. What's the hurry!' [92]

Regardless of how she felt about her 'place', she became more and more settled in her new home. The exhilaration she felt by being at the centre of a burgeoning movement that her charismatic son had created continued to go hand in hand with a sense of uselessness, which fed her tendency toward depression. Within it all, she felt shifts taking place inside herself. At the end of April she wrote:

> It is such a strange place that if one lives here for awhile, however short a time, it finishes by 'getting' you. It is undoubtedly a place of deep suffering for all who live here, in different ways or modes, but it is suffering. There is the frustration of feeling useless. This is my suffering. As time goes on I know that my role is only that of a presence, however much I would like to FEEL useful.

I have just got back from Emmanuel, where there too, I feel inadequate, incapable of praying. I seem to be like a vegetable, just sitting in front of the Lord, not able to utter a word to Him nor to think.

I am sure that your suffering must be much the same, but you have been able to find in your suffering a trust and abandonment. That is what the little St Thérèse had. Just like you, she just trusted, loved and accepted whatever Jesus wanted of her. I think that I can guess a little what you are going through. You don't want me to worry about you, so you don't want me to know how you are nor what you are feeling. I am too close to you not to have been able intuitively to guess much of what is going on ... I am there right close to you, suffering with you, trusting with you, abandoned with you. Jesus loves you with a love of predilection. He is teaching you, drawing you closer to Him at every moment. You have nothing to fear, nothing but just let yourself be loved by Him.

In the two months I have been here I have learnt a lot, and not the way I thought I was going to learn. I am learning to be stripped day by day of what I was and still am. That is the school of L'Arche. I think that all who come here have the same experience in different degrees.

Jock went off last Monday on the Polish pilgrimage with 18 boys and 12 assistants; their departure was really most moving; at 6:30 am Mass, then breakfast, after which Père Thomas blessed each of the cars, Jock gave the signal for the boys to get into the cars, which was done in silence and calm. They left at 7:30 in the spirit needed for such a pilgrimage. They are travelling through Belgium, West and East Germany into Poland, and they go to Cracow, Warsaw and then to the shrine which name I cannot spell.[93] They stay there 2 days and return via Czechoslovakia and Austria. Do pray for them because it is a pilgrimage which could have deep repercussions there and here …[94]

With May came spring sunshine. New assistants kept arriving, and visitors kept Pauline busy. She enjoyed a visit from son Bernard, who worked as an artist and translator, and his wife and two young daughters. By the middle of the month, with her six-month trial period almost at the halfway point, she began to look ahead. Thoughts about the future included plans for redecorating her house in Trosly – a clear sign of the direction toward which she was leaning. She wrote on 19 May:

> I am sad not to have written just lately. I have been overrun with correspondence – just manage to get afloat with letters! And also I have been quite busy doing nothing really worthwhile, but busy just the same. There are many newcomers arriving nearly every day. I try to welcome all of them in turn, inviting them to tea or to lunch; in fact, I am seldom alone for meals …

What do you think! I had a party in my house for 70 assistants. All sat on the floor and sang and sang, also many guitar players. It was great fun, even though a bit tiring because they stayed on until midnight. It was good because I realized how much these young needed relaxation. They just exploded with song. It is an austere life for these youngsters, and they have much responsibility at a very young age.

Every morning I go off with a basket on my arm and do *mes courses* and gossip with some of the old dames like myself. We meet at the general store, the only store in the village, but there are gardens where we get fresh vegetables. The food is far too good, and I'm putting on weight rapidly. Too much bread and butter, which I cannot resist.

I wish you could see the number of our young in the little chapel where they go for silent prayer and stay for a long time before the Blessed Sacrament; it is a real example to me....

We've had nothing but rain and wind. It really has been hard to bear, but believe it or not I haven't had any rheumatism at all. I can even sit on the floor in the chapel without any trouble. Today is lovely – warm sun at last. The flowers and vegetables in my garden are in full bloom. I have radishes and will soon have strawberries, not many, just two rows of them.

I hardly ever see Jock, in fact I've talked with him once since his return from Poland, which was a fortnight ago. He has since preached a retreat in Belgium and has been in Cognac but got back this a.m. early. I may see him during this coming week-end.

I've arranged the big room at the entrance of my house to be a meeting place for the assistants, all white with pretty white curtains in the windows and red drapes, and wicker furniture with red cushions on the floor as most of these young like sitting on the floor. I think that when it is finished it will be a cozy room for them; they can come whenever they feel like it and sing and play guitars. My apartments are quite separate. Two doors keep the sound away, so they do not disturb me at all.

My plans for going home are vague but I think at the end of August. I don't yet know if I'll come back here or not, but I have a sort of feeling that I will. *Il y a des signes qui me font croire que c'est probablement ma vie – maintenant* [There are signs that make me believe that it's probably my life – for now], I'm not yet sure. *Il faut prier pour moi n'est-ce pas* [it's important to pray for me, isn't it]…

By the beginning of June various Vanier plans were beginning to take greater shape. In England, Thérèse, was drawn further into L'Arche. She had taken on the task of finding a suitable house for a L'Arche foundation in Britain. With the help of the Archbishop of Canterbury, an unoccupied vicarage was found in the village of Barfrestone. In Trosly, Pauline continued to be drawn into the spirit of L'Arche. She was increasingly convinced that, in spite of her feeling of inadequacy, L'Arche was the place where she belonged. 'There is something very mysterious about this place; there is much suffering but there is also much peace and also joy at times,' she wrote to her cousin. She continued:

> I continue to be busy because this is the time of many new arrivals; nearly every day there is somebody. Today a Croatian Jesuit arrived and an American nun from Iowa. We have nearly 100 assistants just now; but soon the older ones are going off on holiday so there will be a readjustment. Jock I hardly ever see; this a.m. was a great privilege; he came to breakfast and stayed one whole half hour. I hadn't as long with him for over 2 months. He is off to England tomorrow to see about Thérèse's house. He'll be back for Sunday, so his stay will hardly be 36 hours. He goes to Denmark at the end of the month.
>
> I shall be going to Canada at the end of August. It rather looks as if I would come back here. I think that I can be of some use. My dates are not fixed yet, but I think that I'll be going out about the 27th August and returning here with Jock middle October …'

With summer came more sunshine and a thriving vegetable and flower garden. Pauline picked radishes and lettuce for her meals, adding ruefully that she was continuing to gain weight due to the excellent French bread. On 27 June she wrote a long letter to her cousin outlining the structure of her life as it was unfolding at L'Arche:

> I feel that if I gave you a sort of schedule of one's days' occupation here it might give you an idea of how I spend my time: Up at 6:30 to have my bath because it is the only time there is real hot water. I get back to bed, read my Office and other reading. Breakfast which I prepare, John Dare and sometimes Elizabeth share it with me; we have it in the kitchen. They say my coffee is good. Then I see about the house, talk with my delightful little maid who is a woman of the village, married with four daughters; a good cook and a clean woman. I go do the shopping with my basket, vegetables, groceries. Sometimes one of the boys helps me to carry the basket which can be heavy.
>
> On I go to the Emmanuel Chapel for a quiet prayer, on to the office for the mail, back here for lunch when I usually have one or two of the boys with an assistant … Wash the dishes; people come to see me often after lunch. Then adoration in the chapel. Somebody to tea (an assistant who is depressed is the usual guest), then Mass. Sometimes I go to a foyer for supper to be with the boys, sometimes I have somebody here. Then adoration at 9 pm. On some evenings the assistants meet in

my house…. They sing, play the guitar or talk as they wish. I go to bed at about 10:30.

All sorts of unexpected things happen, people arrive from Paris, want to be shown around, etc., or a boy sick in hospital, so we go into Compiègne to see him, such as it is today. An assistant is ill and comes to my house to convalesce, which was the case last week; that is rather tiring because it means trays, etc. However, it is all part of community life. Some of our young are difficult, very revolted [sic], rebellious about everything, which makes community life somewhat trying at times. But we hope that by being here they may become less rebellious and come to see that the Lord is there. There is also the Mayor that we are trying to bring over to better feelings towards us. He dislikes us intensely. I've invited him to tea with his wife for next Saturday but have not heard if he is coming or not. The boys all call me *la vieille grand-mère* [old grandmother]. I prefer not *vieille*, but they just will use that awful word.

Jock is in Denmark preaching a retreat, not easy in that country. He comes back next Sunday. His problems here are unlimited. I can tell that he has no fun running this place which is becoming so big; they have so many tragic stories amongst them, poor lads. I do love them. But some of them are mighty difficult, not easy to handle. Today I am having a particularly difficult one to lunch …'

By July most of her plans were settled. She decided to have central heating brought into her house with the installation of an oil furnace. Rooms were to be painted as well – but all would wait, as she wrote, 'until my return from Canada'. Of her family, Michel came from Montreal for a visit, and Jean and Thérèse together decided to accept the offer to purchase the house in Barfrestone, Kent. Thérèse made the difficult decision to resign from her work as a clinical haematologist at St Thomas's Hospital in London and to immerse herself in the task of establishing L'Arche in Britain. The light-hearted tone of Pauline's letter on 14 July, suggests a sense of relief at having now decided peacefully on her permanent home:

> My little woman who works for me has a day off, so I've done breakfast as usual, washed dishes, swept the kitchen floor and also the one of the front hall which is large and has black and white tiles which show the dirt, swept the stairs because the assistants who live upstairs bring in a great deal of earth. See how domesticated I am. I rather enjoy it and it is good exercise. I've put on weight as I eat too much of that good bread. There is a lot of walking to do; I suppose I walk about two or three miles a day just going to and fro.
>
> We have a lot of new assistants and many passers-by who spend a day or 24 hours, sometimes even more. A big fat French Canadian priest came through the other day, found me in the garden

where I was weeding. When he saw me he started singing *La belle Canadienne*, much to my embarrassment. I now am known here as *la vieille grand-mère* or *l'ambrassadrice* because so many people kiss me. What it is to be 74 years old. No danger, even the Jesuits give me hugs and kisses ...

My garden is filled with little roses. There is a bower of them. It really is quite lovely; my kitchen garden has lots of lettuce and carrots having had an incredible crop of radishes which we ate most days for weeks. The Lord hides behind a very thick cloud but I know He is there, even if I don't feel anything which I find sometimes a bit difficult ...

As her decision became increasingly clear, she wrote to Sergeant Chevrier, her manservant in Montreal, 'I think God wants me here ... I think I can be of service here in a way that I wouldn't be able to do in Canada.'

In keeping with her initial plan, she returned to Montreal in late August, at the end of her six months' trial period. She sold her house, bade a tearful farewell to her two sons who still remained in Canada, said good-bye to the faithful Sergeant Chevrier, and left again for her new home in France in early October.

An editorial in a daily newspaper based in Toronto, *The Globe and Mail*, noted Pauline's remarkable decision: 'Mrs. Vanier, patroness and co-founder of the Vanier Institute of the Family, chancellor of the University of Ottawa, a great lady with a distinguished record of service to community and country, has given up a well-ordered, comfortable life to join her son, Jean, in work at a community he founded for the mentally retarded near Paris ... We admire her courage and dedication, and applaud her rejection of what her son calls "velvet-cushion Christianity".' [95]

SIX

With Empty Hands 1973-1991

'In the evening of this life, I shall appear before
you with empty hands, for I do not ask you, Lord,
to count my works.'
St Thérèse of Lisieux, Act of Oblation to
Merciful Love, 1895

As L'Arche expanded into more and more communities internationally, Pauline Vanier remained a constant in the house at the centre of the village of Trosly. She took up again with Père Thomas Philippe as her spiritual counsellor.

Her house continued to be a favourite destination for both visitors and assistants. Her presence at the geographical centre of L'Arche gave lustre to the mystique of being Jean Vanier's mother (a reaction she would make fun of in later years, adopting a long face, wide-eyed with mock admiration), but her down-to-earth friendliness and interest in each person put people quickly at ease.

Pauline became known within the community as 'Mamie', a short form of 'Maman'. She became increasingly familiar with the tragic stories of family rejection and institutionalized living that some of the core members had endured, and in spite of the difficult behaviour some of them displayed, she found them more and more loveable and her own fear of them diminishing. On one occasion she was weeping in the chapel when one of the core members took her by the hand and silently led her back to her house. She took this simple and wordless gesture as a sign of unconditional love and acceptance as a member of L'Arche.

But she continued to struggle with the perception of her own uselessness, worrying that she was not sufficiently part of 'the movement': the new, ever-expanding community that was developing. Benedict encouraged her to welcome her 'outside' status – that of being in the community and yet apart from it because there seemed no particular role for her. 'It is a long-term program, but the depths of it are already present in you,' he wrote. 'Allow that new and deeper perception to lead *positively*, and not to discourage you negatively. It will lead you positively, first, by seeing that it is the 'shadow effect' of being near the movement already, and secondly, by allowing, gently and progressively, the correctives that His grace and your own experience will suggest.' [96]

Referring to the clash of personalities that accompanied the fast growth of the community, he added in another letter, 'How often does it not happen that when things go wrong ... it is the presence of a grandmother, a little out of the immediate centre, a little free from the chores and direct responsibilities – and even who doesn't see everything – that can restore confidence and peace. Or again, when there is an axe to grind, it is someone *outside* both axes and grinding – I mean the immediate context of responsibilities and work – who by his or her simple presence can pacify and remove the sting.'

Knowing his mother's extroversion and desire to help anyone who crossed her path, he urged her to take scheduled time for herself: 'I confess I find a trifle disconcerting the inflow of visitors. You may have to give real consideration to having certain periods when you are *not visited* …'[97] He added, in a practical vein, 'Take time off to be sufficiently and really *alone*, in order that the imperfections in your relationship with others have time and place and opportunity to be in truer perspective. Take that time without fear and without exaggeration: it means simply balance and not swinging violently one way or another.' [98]

Her son gradually sensed that she was settling into life at L'Arche, and on 8 November 1975 he wrote, 'I really have the feeling Our Lord has established you in a new form of serenity; not, I mean, to remove all elements of insecurity – that is part and parcel of your life – but, at a deeper level, the assurance of His Presence … Allow that to surface more and more, deepen and spread itself.'

Serenity, however, would never have the upper hand for long. No sooner had she received this affirmation from her Trappist son than she wrote to him with worry that the Pauline who welcomed visitors with warmth and affection was different from the real person she felt herself to be, and therefore she was presenting herself hypocritically to others.

On 25 January 1976 he wrote to her at length about the perception of herself as a hypocrite: the warm welcome she extended to people which seemed to clash with her interior negative sense of who she really was. He reminded her of her particular charism (' your warmth, directness, attention, openness, feeling-with, your presence-to-people') and added:

> Isn't it true that deep down, that's what *He is*? And infinitely so. We are meant to be little – yes, believe it or not – sacraments of His; little walking, breathing, living sacraments. In such ways that something of what He is – warmth, directness, attention, Presence, 'comes through', affects people....Sure – it is based on nature, on a natural gift of spontaneity and of openness, of sharing, and these of course have their shortcomings but because they have their shortcomings (we are human, still weak and 'thick') does not make them cease to be what they are: His gifts, a sharing in His qualities, a reflection of His 'way-of-Being'.

He went on:

> 'Now, what exactly does this gift do? It identifies [others]....You bring them out of their 'anonymity', you make them vibrate as persons, because *you* vibrate as a deeply personal being.... you help to bring them out of [their anonymity]

and their personhood comes into play because of the register of your presence. They start living, they start *being as persons*. You have that gift, it is God's infinitely, but on that humble register, shared by people like yourself. This may help you to realize, too, the importance of the 'nothing' that you do.'

He gave her points to work on: 'openness to everyone, a certain control over excessive sympathy, or on the other hand, antipathy, in Christ's good Name – That will help control the thoughts that you are in hypocrisy; you are not, but you are working towards perfect transparency.' [99]

In early 1976 Jean was stricken with an illness that was diagnosed as amoebic hepatitis and he spent two months in a hospital in Paris and another three months convalescing. When Pauline first arrived at L'Arche she had implicitly expected that Jean would be available to her in a special way. Then, she was continually frustrated by rarely seeing him, and this expectation was gradually replaced with the painful realization that he had his own life and responsibilities – that he had, in a sense, grown away from her. Now, her struggle with emotional detachment was compounded with worry about his health. It was a new phase in Pauline's sense of herself as a mother. Her long-held view of herself as a maternal failure once again came to the fore. In a letter of 20 April Benedict reminded her that she had grown emotionally in her relationship with her children. 'Now, Our Lord asks of you to let that [growth] progress, and moving towards freedom, be proven and confirmed by trial. In other words, to allow the detachment and freedom to be reinforced through trial, to maintain themselves in the face of trial, and to be strengthened. Let His grace see you through. It *is* His grace, and it *will* see you through: to greater freedom yet, and more complete detachment. It is His way, and it is good.' [100]

He went on: 'It is, first, just the surprise of seeing Jock in infirmity; and that means a lot to any mother. Then, the incapacity that is yours to 'do anything about it.' Then again, his particular situation, as head of a community, which has meant for you, so much stripping. You feel, in a way, further from him; but deep down, if you look at it (and you have), nearer to him, but in a totally different way. Having "given him" his independence, nearer him, in a new way. I know this is not without effort, and wrenching, but it is a step to a more complete freedom.' [101]

In March, 1978, Pauline turned 80. The effects of aging were felt with the realization that Père Thomas, whom she had relied on, was slowing down and, she sensed, was less present to her. At the same time, however, the humour that rarely left her still remained in letters to certain long-time friends. The American poet Robert Lax, who had been a friend of the Vaniers since the days of l'Eau Vive in the early 1950s, now resided on the island of Patmos and made occasional visits to Trosly. The playful simplicity with which he approached their friendship found an echo in Pauline's sensibility, especially as she advanced in years. A year after her eightieth birthday she wrote to thank him for a book containing a selection of letters between him and his friend Thomas Merton:

> I am absolutely thrilled to have your book *A Catch of Anti-Letters*. It arrived on the very day of my 81st birthday. I haven't been able to read it as yet but have glimpsed through it. I love your way of addressing one another, quite mad but how really funny. I remember when you were at l'Eau Vive you sometimes would read a few amusing paragraphs from Merton's letters. What a man he was and *you* are quite something yourself.
>
> But - I am really cross with you, that is, I will be cross if you don't come to see us soon. I have the right to say that now that I am an octogenarian – because after all, you never know when I might be recalled to the Father. So there! You *must* come because if I do leave for a better world than this one, I'll take my revenge and tell St Peter about your odious neglect of me. [102]

Her letters to Lax would continue in the same bantering tone, chiding him for not coming to visit her. Two years later she wrote: 'I am slowing down (or is it up?), but at any rate I am beginning to feel the weight of years, and if you want to see me in this world you had better come soon.' She added: 'Jock is crazier than ever - I haven't had a meal with him since December, but have seen him and heard him talk and that he can do with gusto. The handicapped say, "le petit Jean, il parle trop" ["Little Jean talks too much"].' [103]

Still, as she aged, even as her prayer deepened, worry was never far from her. For Lent one year, Benedict replied to a letter in which she had fretted about the necessity of mortifying herself during Lent: 'don't worry too much about "mortifications" (it's pitiful how we are polarized by that!). But, maybe this: trying to avoid *preoccupation*: preoccupation with yourself, and just *openness:* openness to the Lord, to others. A very practical way (and good for all of us!): deliberately, once a day (twice if you can) be total *accueil*, "acceptance", "presence" to someone else. I mean a deliberate effort to follow whoever it is in unconditional acceptance and attention. It is a good "exercise", "practice", because we tend so to bend towards ourselves.' [104] It was an echo of an admonition Pauline had received from Mother Mary of the Cross four decades earlier.

In his Easter letter of 1980 he wrote:

> Forget yourself, and worries and insecurities, and 'how to live'. Forget all that ... and allow it to happen, allow Him *to be* ... I know it takes courage (and determination) and yet it is supreme wisdom, and asked of us, to forget ourselves. It means accepting another world, another reality. We call it *Kingdom*. We could say, too: communion,

> fellowship, covenant. But it means going beyond
> our present, our visible, our tangible, not in the
> sense of denying them, belittling them (even less:
> despising them), but going beyond ... Let Him be,
> and let Him come to us, in that deeper reality, in
> that everlasting setting, in which things passing
> are inserted. *They* pass, but that setting will not,
> does not. [105]

Later that year, Benedict counselled, on a familiar theme, 'Don't be afraid of your temperament. It's yours, with its richness as well as its failings. Never let the negative, the sight of the failings, get the better of thanksgiving, for all it allows you to do, to give, to be.' [106]

In a letter of 2 February 1981 he came back with gentle humour to a leitmotif in Pauline's life during these years: the tug-of-war with her relationship to the visitors and the L'Arche assistants who came to her door: 'Regarding what you say, that you are not 'present' to people when they come and visit you and 'begrudge' it when they don't. The first thing is to have a good laugh, because if you are happy neither when alone nor with others, surely you are going to have to go into space! So, a good laugh is the first thing. The second is to recognize our misery.' He added, on a playful note: 'Here is a little tip, contemplation-wise. We buy big bags of Quaker's Puffed Wheat. If you take a good bowl, you feel lightheaded, if you take a second, you drift gently toward the ceiling ... Don't blame St

John of the Cross for not speaking of such matters; they weren't invented in his day.' [107]

The early 1980s brought a recurrence of the eye problem that had plagued Pauline intermittently for nearly fifty years. From now until her death her ability to read and write would gradually diminish. For prayer, Benedict recommended a mantra-like form of contemplation, what he described as 'a new way of learning prayer': a slow repetition of the Hail Mary, with a prayerful focus on the word "Blessed": "Blessed art thou….Blessed is the Fruit…"' 'All the mystery of God's saving grace and love is present in those humble words that open us to His Spirit,' [108] he wrote. Benedict was to return to this form of prayer in his letters, expanding it to include the Divine Praises that are recited at Benediction: 'Blessed be God, Blessed be His Holy Name….': 'When we are 'stuck' it is a good practice, very gently and slowly, to let those Divine Praises come up to our lips and our hearts. It gets us out of ourselves and on the track of praise and gratuity, and that is a tremendous step not just in life, but in prayer.' [109]

Her difficulty in setting the personal boundaries necessary in order to take quiet time for herself was complicated, even as she moved into her mid-eighties, by the recurring feeling of hypocrisy. Benedict wrote:

'… when a young person comes to visit you, forget everything, except that that person belongs to God (even if he or she does not know it) and is on

a pilgrimage to Him, living here in a time of trial
– of glory to Him. That will give you the words to
say – often to say *nothing*, or nearly nothing, just
to appreciate that person at his/her real value. A
value that comes from Him, and is there, always.
It may seem nothing, to say or write that, but it is
everything! It dictates our attitude, our presence,
and these will say the rest … We are more in truth,
and what more could we want? There is often
little to say, but a lot to communicate and to con-
firm, just in our attitude and in our presence.' [110]

Two years later, he wrote on the same theme:

You worry about what people *think* and what you
are. Just remember what we said: imperfections
in our motivations are imperfections – they do
not make our actions *bad*. They represent *dust*,
absence of transparency. They are terrain for effort
and purification, but they do not 'blacken' everything we do and all that we are. The Lord Himself
takes in hand that purification as well you know.
That lack of transparency can make us moan, for
sure – and rightly so; yet we shouldn't be too dismayed at its presence. Making effort to be more
open, more *accueillant* [welcoming] (to everyone
and everything, but more especially to hope and
confidence) is always possible and always asked
of us. But let's not be dismayed or discouraged

because there is work to be done and better transparency to come about. [111]

When she wrote of the 'void' and 'emptiness' in her
spiritual life, Benedict answered: 'Remember all the
faculties – even the most spiritual – have their 'substra-
tum', their roots, in our body, our 'neurology' – and so it
is not surprising that with age, even outside of specific
illness, there will be a 'slowing down', and absence of
'vibration' – a sort of 'void, 'no reaction'. That is normal; do less, do little, but do well. Be really present
to people less long, less frequently. Yes, it takes trust,
'abandon'; you just can't do more. Don't worry – the
Lord does not expect that 'more', but offer our abandon and trust. He is there, in our 'void" [112]

Some letters to Robert Lax during these years refer
to a 'black tunnel' that surfaced from time to time. In
an undated letter she wrote, 'I am neither St John of the
Cross nor Merton to think it was a mystical experience.
I'm afraid that it was, alas, only my very bad nervous
system. Patmos sounds heavenly, and I must admit that
I would gladly exchange it with Trosly, especially at this
season when the skies are grey and the air so humid.' [113]

In another letter she wrote, 'You rejoice whenever
you think of me. That is a comforting feeling, but I'm
getting to be a pretty dried up old creature and need to
be revived.' [114] Her main responsibility, of welcoming
new assistants, remained, and guests from outside the
community continued to call. She often greeted them
at the door with an all-enveloping bear hug. Some

became close friends, and to them she was known as 'Ma V'. The former Canadian Prime Minister Pierre Trudeau and his three sons came to call. The parents of assistants, to whom she was 'Madame Vanier', also visited, one of them, an American, remarking, 'She doesn't act like a madame at all!' [115] The priest and writer Henri Nouwen, who later joined the Daybreak L'Arche community in Canada, stayed with her for several months. Their talks reminded her of Père Pichon and her mother's devotion, through him, to the Heart of Jesus as an expression of God's merciful love. At Pauline's urging, and inspired by her passion, Nouwen's book *Heart Speaks to Heart* was eventually published in 1989.

She wrote to Benedict that she was drinking a lot of tea, and from across the Atlantic he recognized the veiled meaning of this short message: a tendency toward excessive socializing and entertaining, followed by exhaustion and depression. 'Be careful not to overdo,' he cautioned her. 'Sure, there are many assistants you "have to invite" – but be careful. Limit things according to your strength; don't overdo. Do less and do well.' [116]

Eventually she set up Thursday night prayer sessions with some of the assistants. She had heard of an English Benedictine monk by the name of John Main, who had founded a monastery in Montreal. Using a form of Christian meditation adapted from an Eastern technique, he had begun praying with groups in this way. Using John Main's method, she played a cassette recording of a talk by him and, with only a candle for light, the group spent an hour in meditation. In the community, she took a particular interest in a new foyer called La Forestière, which had been built for people who had physical as well as mental handicaps.

Worries increased as her physical strength diminished and her world grew narrower. She worried that, having co-founded the Vanier Institute of the Family, she was guilty of hypocrisy because both her married sons, Bernard and Michel, had become divorced from their wives. She wrote pages to Father Benedict of what she called 'poubelle' (garbage), litanies of her failings: she became haughty and demanding over small matters such as inelegant meal presentations; her spontaneity, once considered charming, now sometimes burst out in flashes of anger; she grew depressed and impatient in the face of her waning energy; she sometimes fell into self-pity at no longer being the centre of attention. She worried from time to time that she did not fit in at L'Arche and that she was somehow at fault for being a failure.

Her son responded with soothing reminders and more profoundly, he reminded her of the spiritual attitude of 'abandonment' that she had taken upon herself: the mental act of letting go and 'handing over' of herself to the mercy of God.

By 1986 she could no longer read or see well enough to write. She relied on cassette tapes for reading material, and the generosity of assistants to whom she dictated her letters. The damp cold of the winters in northern France seeped into her bones, aggravating the arthritis in her back, and the unremitting grey skies tended to lower her spirits. She wrote to Robert Lax that although L'Arche 'is a peaceful place it is in some ways very super active and I get so fed up with the goings and comings. Here am I a grumbly old woman. Actually, I am very happy here but the old carcass is beginning to creak and moan and that makes me cross.'[117] Inability to read meant that she was now more dependent on others.

Commiserating, Benedict wrote:

> I have no illusions about the 'tryingness' of this time for yourself – I mean, without reading and writing, and all the element of sharing, of nourishing, of affirming, that is wrapped up in them. If it is stripping, which is obvious, it is also preparing for a new and even simpler reliance and communication with Him. Not so much in words, for sure, as in attitude and in silence. God IS, and our attitude and silence say more than our words. You will say that your attitude is not always edifying! I believe you – and He understands it all. That attitude and silence is…not overnight success. He IS – let's complete it – He is LOVE.[118]

He advised returning to the simple contemplative repetition of 'Blessed', for which she would need no visual help: 'It is beautiful, too, to see that it is the same word that comes back, again and again, in the Beatitudes: "Blessed are …" – they are to share in the Blessedness of God Himself.'[119]

In letters to Lax she gave accounts in detail of Jean's travels as he moved about the globe visiting L'Arche communities and participating in dialogues and retreats. 'Jock is crazier than ever,' was a common comment, combining bewilderment and admiration. 'How have I produced such a bird?' she asked in one letter, giving a one-sided answer: 'Of course it had a father!' [120] Her worry as a mother was evident in nearly every letter: on 6 May 1988, in the midst of the Palestinians' first intifada, she wrote, 'Jean is leaving on the 14th for the West Bank. So say a prayer for him; I don't like that place for him.' [121] And always, after the list of Jean's destinations: a variation of 'I only hope that he is really doing God's work.'

Anxieties about herself from earlier years manifested themselves in new ways; she feared loneliness and panicked whenever she was left alone. She sometimes said she was afraid to die, but at other times complained that God had forgotten to come for her. As her hearing, too, began to fail, she feared that she would become senile and an impossible burden on the community. Still, humour sometimes surfaced. Teasing Robert Lax about his promise to visit her, she wrote, 'If I can make you feel that you should come here, I only wish that feeling could become concrete. If you don't come soon and I am called away to the next world, you will have a deep remorse and I'll haunt you.' [122]

She seemed to enjoy reminding Lax of the extremity of her old age: 'I don't understand your jokes as quickly as I used to, but go on sending me some of your crazy jokes; they help the old girl'. [123] And in reply to an indecipherable inscription in a book he had sent: 'Well, the dotted [inscription] intrigued me, but it is I should gather something from your subconscious or mine. It is a sort of conundrum, a compliment to my intelligence, but I am not sure you are right to have supposed that.' [124]

A month before her ninetieth birthday, thanking him for a book of poems he had sent, she took crotchety advantage of her advanced years: 'The poems are intriguing to look at; so far, I've found nobody intelligent enough to interpret them to me. But I'm praying that that person will suddenly turn up. I'm grateful for the book, but I am hoping for an autograph which I can stick in so as to remember the author. Please not one in your abstract style, consisting of dots which were so frustrating for me to decipher. Remember that, when ninety, one hasn't the same possibility of delving in the abstract.' [125]

Humour revealed itself in other ways as well. When she managed to bend down sufficiently to tie her shoe laces, she flashed a V-for-victory sign. When homecare help was requested from the nearby town of Pierrefonds and a male nurse presented himself as the person sent to bathe her, she gave a momentary start, and then laughed and shrugged off her feminine modesty. Lying on a hospital gurney one year, laid low by a sprained back, she howled with laughter when an attendant remarked to her, 'You must have been a beautiful woman at one time.' And again to Robert Lax, in one of her endless requests for a visit from him: 'Remember that I am not getting any younger and how long shall I remain lucid? So try and come before I become ga-ga. Or I might leave the planet.' [126]

On 28 March 1988 she turned ninety. Toward the end of the birthday celebration she became overwhelmed by the day's emotion and began to weep. One of the core members, a mute thirty-year-old man by the name of Loïc Proffit, who was the size of a six-year-old child, climbed onto her lap. Leaning over, he raised her chin and rested his cheek against hers. She later acknowledged that recognizing and receiving this gesture as a gift of the heart demanded an inner poverty and openness. Increasingly, she was identifying with the handicapped people around her, and in fact had become one of them.

Her life had now been taken to its extreme, and there was nothing left but simplicity, weakness, and waiting. Thanking Robert Lax for another book of poems, called *21 Pages*, she wrote: 'I am fortunate enough at the present moment to have a friend who can read you. She read *21 Pages* – searching, waiting, finding. How strange that in the course of our conversation I said to you that you should write about waiting. It is when my friend read the *21 Pages* that I discovered waiting. And I also understood darkness, light, black, white. So much has been illuminated in me. Thank you to have let me delve within the mystery you are.' She continued: 'I wish I were a poet, able to exchange with you the mystery that we both live. I think that I had better not try to go further. I just want you to know that you already know that our friendship is precious to me and that my love is deep.' [127]

The end came quickly. On Thursday 21 March 1991, one of the assistants found her curled up in bed, sobbing and in physical agony. At the hospital in Compiègne, tests revealed intestinal cancer, and she was operated on the next day. On Saturday 23 March, full of tubes and surrounded by machines, she opened her eyes briefly and recognized Jean at her side, and then she lapsed into unconsciousness and died shortly afterward. It was five days before her ninety-third birthday and the day before Palm Sunday, the beginning of Holy Week. Her funeral Mass in Trosly was celebrated on 25 March, the anniversary of her son Benedict's ordination to the priesthood.

Pauline Vanier's body was returned to Canada on a Canadian armed services plane, and on 3 April another funeral Mass took place in Notre Dame Basilica in Quebec City. The Canadian flag was draped over her casket. Her body was later buried beside that of her husband in the memorial chapel of the Citadel in Quebec City, the home of the Canadian francophone regiment, where Georges Vanier was once the commander. On the stone over Georges Vanier's grave was inscribed the first two lines of Psalm 121: *J'étais dans la joie quand on m'a dit: Allons dans la maison du Seigneur* ['I rejoiced when I heard them say: Let us go to God's house']. These words formed the Introit of the Mass for the Fourth Sunday of Lent, the day he died. The stone over Pauline Vanier's grave carries the remainder of the verse from the same psalm: *Et maintenant devant tes portes notre marche prend fin* ['And now our feet are standing within your gates'].

◄──◄◄◄◄◄◄══════►►►►►►─►

During his stay at L'Arche in Trosly in 1985, Henri Nouwen reflected on the teaching of Père Thomas: 'It is not so much the ability to think, to reflect, to plan, or to produce that makes us different from the rest of creation, but the ability to trust. It is the heart that makes us truly human. [The heart] is the place where all is one in God, the place where we truly belong, the place from which we come and to which we always yearn to return.' [128] This was Georges and Pauline Vanier, together and singly: yearning for God, alive in the world and always at the heart of the Church, the life of the Spirit emanating from them; the light shining through the broken vessel.

After Georges's death in 1967, his cardiologist wrote to Pauline, 'In truth, your husband lived with God and by God. The presence of God was expressed in his gestures and words, with, of course, the utmost discretion and disarming simplicity. Is holiness anything other than this intimate and constant life with God?' [129] He could have written similarly about Pauline, for the 'intimate and constant life with God' was the essence of their married life together.

Notes

1   The Carmel in Hitchin, Hertfordshire.
2   Georges P. Vanier Archives, Library and Archives Canada, Box 106, file 1.
3   *Story of a Soul*, trans. by John Clarke OCD, ICS Publications, Washington, DC, 1975, page 150.
4   *Ibid.*, page 151.
5   Georges P. Vanier Archives, Library and Archives Canada, Box 106, file 1.
6   Private correspondence.
7   *Story of a Soul*, trans. by John Clarke OCD, ICS Publications, 1975, pages 187-8.
8   1 Cor. 12:31.
9   Wisdom 6:7.
10 Psalm 40:7-8.
11 9 May 1944, Georges P. Vanier Archives, Library and Archives Canada, Box 103, file 9.
12 Psalm 119, Grail translation.
13 2 Cor. 12:10.
14 *The Story of a Soul*, page 277.
15 1 Cor. 27.
16 1 Peter 2:10.
17 Obituary of Roger Clutton SJ, Archives of the British Province of the Society of Jesus.
18 Katharine Kendall, *Spiritual Teaching of Father Steuart*, Burns Oates, London 1952, page 67.
19 *Ibid.*, page 87.
20 Vanier private papers, 28 August 1938.
21 Box 11, file 26, 16 February 1939.
22 Undated, Georges P. Vanier Fonds, Library and Archives Canada, Box 106 file 10.
23 On 10 May 1941 Deputy Fuhrer Rudolf Hess flew to Scotland in a purported attempt to negotiate peace with the British. He was immediately arrested.
24 At St Thérèse's canonization, on 17 May 1925, Pope Pius XI spoke of her path of spiritual childhood.
25 Box 12 file 5, 23 December 1942.
26 Private correspondence, 31 March 1943.
27 Box 14 file 20, 1 September 1943.

28 24 August 1943, Box 14, file 20.
29 Box 15 file 26, 28 March 1944.
30 Box 15 file 26, 30 March 1944.
31 Box 15 file 26, 24 August 1944.
32 Box 106 file 17, 11 September 1944.
33 Box 17 file 34.
34 Box 106 file 19, 8 June 1945.
35 Box 106 file 18, 21 April 1945.
36 Box 106 file 18, 30 August 1945.
37 7 January 1946, Georges P. Vanier Fonds, Box 106 file 25.
38 Father Benedict Vanier, private papers.
39 Private papers.
40 Box 23, file 45.
41 Father Benedict Vanier, private papers.
42 17 November 1946, Georges P. Vanier Fonds, Box 18 file 1.
43 15 December 1946, *ibid.*
44 Easter 1947, *ibid.*
45 Murray Ballantyne, 8 November 1946, Georges P. Vanier Fonds, Box 20 file 29.
46 Murray Ballantyne, 23 February 1950, Georges P. Vanier Fonds, Box 20 file 29.
47 10 July 1951, Box 21 file 14.
48 1 May 1947, Box 107, file 4.
49 23 February 1952, Box 21 file 33.
50 20 October 1946, Box 107, file 1.
51 23 May 1947, Box 107, file 5.
52 Henri J.M. Nouwen, Foreword, *The Contemplative Life* by Thomas Philippe OP, The Crossroad Publishing Company, 1990.
53 Georges P. Vanier Fonds, Box 23, file 29.
54 Georges P. Vanier Fonds, Box 20 file 30.
55 *Ibid.*
56 'L'Eau Vive' by Thomas Philippe OP, Georges P. Vanier Fonds, Box 107 file 5.
57 12 September 1953, Georges P. Vanier Fonds, Box 22 file 13.
58 Arthur Biddle, ed., *When Prophecy Still had a Voice: The Letters of Thomas Merton and Robert Lax*, The University of Kentucky Press, Lexington KT, 2001, page 119.
59 *Ibid.*, page 120.
60 *Ibid.*, page 121.
61 Undated, 1954, private papers.
62 Eugene Boylan, *The Spiritual Life of the Priest*, The Newman Press, Westminster, Maryland, page 22.

63   Georges P. Vanier Fonds, Box 101, file 2.

64   *Ibid.*

65   St Margaret Mary Alacoque was a seventeenth-century French nun who had visions of Jesus revealing his heart. These experiences led to the devotion to the Sacred Heart.

66   *Ibid.*

67   *Ibid.*

68   9 March 1964, private papers.

69   Interview with the author, 19 May 1987.

70   28 August 1958.

71   22 August 1959, Box 101, file 3.

72   6 February 1959, Box 101 file 3.

73   Georges P. Vanier, *Only to Serve*, University of Toronto Press, Toronto, 1970, pages 3-5.

74   Remarks on receiving an honourary LLD from Laurentian University, Sudbury, 27 October 1961.

75   Georges P. Vanier Fonds, Box 103 file 8.

76   Box 110 file 1.

77   Box 110 file 5.

78   8 July 1964, Box 110, file 5.

79   Peter Buckley, *Canadian Press*, 7 October 1965.

80   15 August 1958, private papers.

81   13 August 1963, private papers.

82   14 November 1966, private papers.

83   Box 21 file 14.

84   *Ibid.*

85   Undated, Benedict Vanier, private papers.

86   Box 112, file 7.

87   22 January 1970, Box 114, file 1.

88   Private papers.

89   Elizabeth Buckley and John Dare were young assistants whom Pauline had known in Montreal.

90   *Vanier: Soldier, Diplomat, Governor General,* by Robert Speaight.

91   Raphaël Simi was one of the two men Jean Vanier originally moved in with in 1964.

92   14 April 1972. Private correspondence.

93   Czestochowa.

94   A L'Arche community was eventually established in Poland.

95   *The Globe and Mail*, 2 March 1972.

96   undated.

97   22 January 1974, private correspondence.

98   3 December 1973, private correspondence.

99   25 January 1976.

100 20 April 1976.
101 20 April 1976, private correspondence.
102 7 April 1979, St Bonaventure's Archives.
103 7 March 1980, St Bonaventure's Archives.
104 Undated.
105 Easter, 1980.
106 1 October 1980.
107 2 February 1981.
108 10 September 1982.
109 13 January 1986.
110 Christmas 1982.
111 7 November 1984.
112 5 March 1983.
113 Undated, 19 February.
114 Undated.
115 Elizabeth Buckley, interview with author, 25 August, 2009.
116 25 September 1984, private correspondence.
117 16 February, year undated, St Bonaventure Archives.
118 30 November 1986.
119 30 November 1987.
120 1 November 1989.
121 6 May 1988.
122 7 November, undated.
123 24 February 1986.
124 7 November 1979.
125 8 February 1988.
126 1 November 1989.
127 20 November 1989.
128 Henri J.M. Nouwen, *The Road to Daybreak*, Doubleday, New York, 1988, page 48.
129 Dr. Paul David, July, 1967, quoted in *In Weakness, Strength*, Griffin Press Limited, Toronto, 1969, page 7.

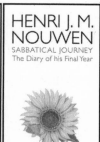